Chris Wells studied medicine [illegible]).
After four years in Canada, [illegible] d
commenced working at the Centre for Pain Relief, Walton
Hospital, in 1979. He became Director of the Centre in 1983. The Clinic is one of the largest of its kind in the world, and is famous for its wide range of treatments, and in particular for pioneering many new forms of therapy. It was the first NHS clinic to use acupuncture, in 1970; also, many nerve blocks and other treatments for cancer pain were used for the first time in this unit.

Dr Wells established the Pain Management Programme in 1982 with Dr Eric Ghadiali. It was the first programme of its type in the UK, and has been running continuously since. Well over 1000 patients have passed through the Programme, many gaining permanent improvements in their quality of life. He has written numerous scientific papers on all aspects of pain relief, from pain programmes to cancer research, several chapters of books for specialists in pain relief, articles in the popular press and consumer magazines, and is in constant demand as a lecturer both at home and abroad. He is married with two children, and the family hobby is horseriding, which itself at times can be a painful occupation!

Former award-winning journalist Graham Nown is the author of more than 30 non-fiction books, in addition to broadcasting and writing for television. He is married to children's writer Sylvana Nown. They have one daughter and live in Southport, on the North West coast.

Introduction

The Price of Pain

'It became more than something physical. Rather than taking up the space somewhere between my foot and lower back, the pain took up my whole life. I didn't meet people. I spent a lot of time in bed. It not only took me over, it affected all the people around me ...'

At some time in our lives we all endure the agony of pain. If we are lucky, it may only be passing. When it persists, it can turn into a primeval monster in our midst, breaking up families, causing depression, financial hardship or divorce.

Prolonged pain has the power to crush our self-confidence and lead us to lose a sense of who we are. It is rather like being trapped in an endlessly revolving door. At its extreme, sufferers may even be driven to attempt suicide.

As one medical study put it: 'pain is not just an epidemic, but a major social problem.' It inflicts terrible damage at a cost which cannot be counted in pounds or dollars – disrupting life, destroying relationships, cutting us off from family and friends.

Anyone with a blinding migraine attack or nagging back pain will know that it is impossible to function normally – to concentrate at work, take the kids to the park, watch a movie or enjoy dinner in a restaurant. Pain becomes the centre of every working day, shouldering aside everything of value and importance.

One patient, John Ball, explained:

> 'I didn't want to do anything. My family life went out of the window. I just sat in a chair like an old zombie. If my grandchildren came to the house, I would vanish upstairs and lie on the bed to get out of the way.'

Pain makes demands of us and puts us under pressure. As it progresses, our lives have to be organised around it. Even reality becomes distorted.

Here's how it affected Philippa, a photographer suffering from sciatica, originally caused by a slipped disc:

> 'The biggest effect is social isolation. You don't believe you can go out and meet people any more. You don't believe you have anything to offer them. In a sense, your pain becomes your identity. There is nothing else to speak about. All your experience is about pain and being in bed surrounded by four walls. It becomes a self-perpetuating cycle.'

Allowing pain to take us over totally is not unusual. John, who suffers from osteo-arthritis, describes how pain changed his outlook:

> 'I didn't want to socialize with people at all. Before my illness I was a friendly, hale-fellow-well-met sort of guy. Then, I just withdrew into my shell. The pain was really severe. Because of it, I slowly began to lose the use of the rest of my body.'

If any of those symptoms sound familiar, then the chances are that you are suffering from prolonged or chronic pain. Eventually whatever illness you have becomes secondary to the pain itself. In addition you may suffer from loss of sleep, constant tiredness, digestive disorders and drug dependency. As every sufferer knows, the agony of pain is likely being on a treadmill. The longer it persists, the more the edges of life become blurred, leaving little hope to cling to.

In Britain, only about a tenth of people suffering from back pain ever mention it to their family doctor – and yet there are still 2.2 million back pain consultations a year.

More than 30 per cent of diabetics have been found to suffer chronic pain and half of them do not consider complaining to their doctor. There is no doubt that all of them – and thousands of others – are in great discomfort, but they simply feel that little can be done.

Traditional methods of treating pain are often ineffectual. It is perhaps not surprising that a 1978 survey of American general practitioners revealed that many lose interest in those long-term disorders for which tablets offer little relief and the chances of successful treatment are slight.

The problem also lies within ourselves. We have been conditioned through advertizing, television and magazines to expect a pill for every symptom we suffer. It is not a healthy outlook to have – for us or our society. Medicine may have made great strides, but miracles are not yet in sight.

One of the problems of pain is that it produces a dependence on doctors and drugs. When we sit down in the surgery and complain of a headache or backache, what we are really doing is trying to hand over our pain to the doctor and ask him to take it away.

This brings us to the first lesson of pain relief, and it may come as a surprise: the only effective way to overcome pain is to do something about it ourselves. Hoping for a medical magic wand to wave it away is not the solution.

Pain researchers find that people who suffer most from chronic pain are those who hand the problem to their doctor and settle for the aspirin-and-rest approach. Those who suffer least are those who exercise regularly, making an effort to change their outlook and place pain low on their scale of importance.

Accepting the burden of your own pain and resolving to do something about it is a big step to take. Some sufferers trail their pain from doctor to doctor and try countless prescriptions in the hope that someone else will take the agony away from them. Others, after years of discomfort, are even reluctant to give up their pain. They can no longer visualise life without it.

Of course, it is wonderful news if you can find a pain killer which completely removes the pain and allows you to resume normal living. The sad truth, however, is that life rarely runs so smoothly. It is probably safe to say that most people taking drugs for chronic pain find that the effects of them eventually wear off. It is quite common for pain sufferers to take a dozen or more pain killers a day and still have pain and limited activity. To add to their problems, they will probably have to cope with the unpleasant side effects of withdrawal if they try to discontinue them. Thousands of people find themselves caught in this cruel trap and turn in desperation to different doctors who, in turn, offer different drugs.

The lesson underlines the first rule of pain relief: try to do something about it yourself, rather than leave it to others. In the long march of medicine, it is a new concept, but results encourage the view that self-help may be the most hopeful pain treatment of the future.

While it is not advisable to stop any kind of treatment without medical advice, recent pain research has shown that drugs may actually inhibit the body's own ability to get better. Total reliance on drugs is unwise when we have resources within our bodies that may fight pain more effectively, with no unpleasant effects.

One patient, John, described the drawback of drugs:

> 'I have had headaches all my life but, for the last ten or eleven years, they have been almost constant. A pressure pain is with me when I go to bed and it is still there when I wake up in the morning. It is so long since I have been free from pain that I no longer know what it is like to be different.
>
> 'My doctor prescribed tranquillisers, but they just made me very tired. The problem became worse. I was unable to do the things I wanted to do. As a result, my anxiety increased. When I mentioned this to my doctor, he told me to keep taking the tablets.
>
> 'Eventually, I decided to stop. The pain is still there, but I feel more alive as a person. More ready to do something to help myself.'

Five people in six in Britain take pain killers when they feel pain. It has been estimated that 70 per cent of patients who turn to pain killers still suffer terrible pain. The scope of the problem, and the misery it causes, is now so vast and commonplace that it becomes almost difficult to comprehend.

A health study in Britain revealed that eleven and a half per cent of the population suffer chronic pain: that is, pain that occurs at some occasion on every day for more than three months. When the survey was carried out among members of the public visiting patients in hospital, 15 per cent of the visitors admitted having chronic pain themselves.

Wherever we live, or however we live, pain has become a disabling scourge on society. It makes no distinction between wealth, race or social standing. Millions of ordinary people throughout the world suffer silently because they believe nothing can be done to help them.

The desperation of a patient, Alan, sums up their feelings:

> 'I was on twenty tablets a day,' he said, 'but nothing was working. I would have tried anything to get rid of the pain. Anything at all.'

As many as 30 per cent of people in the United States are thought to suffer chronic pain. In fact, more than 50 million Americans are partly or completely disabled by pain for a few days each month – a loss of 700 million working days of a year. And some of them may never recover from it. Add to this the cost of health care bills, compensation payments and, in many cases, attorneys' fees and the price of pain soars to almost $100 billion a year.

In Britain, the most common symptom doctors have to deal with is headache. About 30 per cent of the population suffers from headache at some time during any one year. Twenty one per cent of otherwise healthy people are said to complain of back pain in any one-month period.

A nationwide survey conducted by *Which? Way To Health* indicated that there are probably as many as five million chronic pain sufferers in Britain. More than half said that chronic pain had affected their ability to work or lead a normal life.

The largest group of sufferers (33 per cent) were those with neck and back pain, a condition which costs the National Health Service £193 million a year.

Seventy per cent of pain sufferers in Britain take pain killing drugs every day to seek some form of relief. The number, which is approaching crisis proportions, indicates that prolonged medication is ineffective in controlling pain and allowing increased activity. The old cliche 'keep taking the tablets' is simply not enough.

According to the Arthritis and Rheumatism Council, back

pain accounts for around 20 million lost working days each year. Statistics like these are plentiful: in America it has been calculated that five per cent of the cost of a first-class letter goes towards covering the wages of US Postal Service mailmen off work with back pain.

Pain is the biggest drain on a nation's resources. In the State of Washington, for example, 36 per cent of the state's compensation payments go to patients suffering from lower back pain. In California, hospital treatment for back ailments alone costs around $80 million a year. Figures such as these tell merely a tiny part of the story. Only those who suffer pain – from migraine to backache, or diabetes to dreaded forms of cancer – can truly understand its demoralizing effects.

In Europe and America more than 200 times the amount allocated to pain research is spent on pain killers, an annual drugs bill of $2 billion in the USA alone. However, advances in pain management and research in the past 20 years have proved that relief can be achieved which does not necessarily involve increasing drug dosages or other medical treatments. Learning to cope with pain and increasing our activities, with less reliance on medicine and doctors, is sometimes the best way forward.

The first practical step on the road to conquering pain is to understand its nature and the mechanics of how it works.

There are essentially two types of pain. *Acute pain* is the kind of reaction we feel when we burn our finger, or drop something heavy on our foot. Its purpose is to give us useful warning that we have hurt ourselves or suffered tissue damage. Acute pain is positive. We all need it at some time in our lives. It is the sensation that makes us jerk our finger from the flame or move away from danger rapidly.

Acute pain is practical and protective – so much so that it is actually extremely harmful if we are unable to feel it. There are unusual cases of people who do not feel acute pain at all.

Someone who has been in severe pain for 20 years might envy them, but they are unfortunate. Without the sensation of acute pain they might be unaware they have a broken limb, or a serious burn, which could otherwise have been avoided. There are occasions when acute pain is a distinct advantage in our daily lives.

Chronic pain – pain that simply doesn't go away – can have many causes. Often, an accident, injury or some physical reason can trigger the pain; this might either be untreatable, or treatment might fail. Often in chronic pain the amount of discomfort seems to far exceed the physical cause. It is well accepted that chronic pain is an emotional experience and that psychological factors play a large part in maintaining the discomfort felt.

The pain sufferer, however, is left with a pain which is both long-term and debilitating. The pain is not useful because it is not an indication of minute-by-minute tissue damage. There is no advantage in sufferers seeking instant medical advice because treatment is not going to cure them. More importantly, rest and prolonged medication is not going to be helpful either: it is only liable to lead to further problems, rather than resolving the symptoms.

Chronic pain sufferers may have any one of a dozen or so conditions or diseases. They can range from arthritis and back problems to diabetes and include a host of other diseases, such as multiple sclerosis or shingles. What they all have in common is that the pain is both long-term and disabling. The most important point to remember about chronic pain is that it serves no useful purpose at all.

Dr Richard Chapman and Dr John Bonica, of the University of Washington School of Medicine who carried out the American study, revealed three important findings about the difference between acute and chronic pain:

- Mental attitudes play a great part in someone suffering long-term pain.
- Surroundings and social relationships affect chronic pain sufferers more than acute pain sufferers.
- The link between the source of the pain and the pain itself actually becomes weaker as chronic pain progresses. In other words, the body almost forgets the original illness or injury but continues to generate pain messages. The pain begins to almost acquire a life of its own.

By bearing these points in mind and resolving to work on them by following a pain relief programme, great strides can be made towards mastering the pain in your own body.

The self-help pain relief programme in this book is based on successful methods used by the Pain Relief Clinic at Walton Hospital, Liverpool – one of the biggest in the world – and research carried out at the Pain Relief Research Institute adjoining the hospital. Strongly against carrying out experiments involving animals, the Institute is the first of its kind in the world devoted entirely to research into chronic pain in people. It has become an international focus of pain research, sharing discoveries and passing on training in pain-relief techniques. With a wide scope of projects and thorough medical investigations, its results have brought real relief to patients all over the world and the promise of new hope to many more.

Twenty nine per cent of patients on the Pain Management 'Self-Help' Programme are able to go back to work after previously being unable to work at all. Many more resume an active social life and enjoy the company of family and friends without the demands that pain once placed upon them.

The out-patient programme at Walton runs for four weeks and consists of activities and therapies specifically designed to help patients cope better with their pain. It is not a miracle cure and patients are told that their pain is unlikely to have disappeared by the end of the programme. What they may hope to achieve is reduced pain levels and a feeling of being less distressed and restricted by their pain. There is also every hope they may become more active and confident, less reliant on tablets and other physical methods of pain relief and feel generally better and more in control.

Most patients who attend the Pain Relief Clinic see it as a last resort. Often, they have attended several doctors and consultants and received a variety of drugs, with little success. If their pain had had one simple cause, it would have been treated and cured long ago. Like many chronic pain sufferers who have found no relief, it has become a complex process which responds more readily to the range of therapies offered in the programme.

For them, there is no other treatment, long term, which is likely to work. It is a last opportunity to gain control over their pain and improve the quality of their lives.

The steps outlined in the following chapters can help you develop the same ability to cope with long-term pain through physical and mental exercise.

Chronic pain has very important psychological as well as physical aspects. What you think about, how you behave, how other people treat you, your attitudes and feelings can *all* exert very strong influences on your perception of pain. These psychological aspects can act almost like a volume control, turning the volume up or down on the pain, depending on what you are thinking about or doing.

The 'behavioural' approach to pain management concentrates more on the psychological rather than the physical aspects of pain and provides an effective way of helping many people who suffer with chronic pain.

The Programme, which has run continuously since 1983, was devised by Consultant Anaesthetist Dr Chris Wells and

Consultant Neuropsychologist Dr Eric Ghadiali. Treatment is provided by a multi-disciplinary team of professionals, including medical staff, a Clinical Psychologist, Occupational Therapists, Physiotherapists, a Dance Instructor, a Dietician, a T'ai Chi Instructor, a Healer, voluntary workers and 'pain graduates' – patients who have successfully attended the Programme and return to provide extra assistance. All members of the team have extensive experience in the management and treatment of chronic pain.

The aims of the Programme, reflected in this book, are to:

1 Increase daily activities.
2 Increase physical fitness: power, endurance and flexibility.
3 Learn relaxation skills.
4 Reduce distress and disability.
5 Increase self-confidence and ability to function, and improve coping skills.
6 Eliminate unhelpful beliefs about pain.
7 Reduce addictive or unnecessary drugs.
8 Improve understanding of pain.
9 Improve sleep and reduce sedatives.
10 Eliminate aids, such as corsets, sticks, collars and wheelchairs.
11 Return to work where appropriate.
12 Reduce dependence on doctors and reduce Health Service utilisation.

Pain is expensive, both in personal terms and the welfare of society. But the price is high only until you do something about it yourself. Once that decision is made, work, family and personal relationships become a possibility again.

In the words of Margaret, a car crash victim:

> 'I have realized that my life has not come to an end. There are all kinds of things I can do and goals I can achieve. I can cope with the pain by removing myself from it. I am no longer a prisoner. For the first time, I have a sense of freedom.'

Breaking the chains of pain is not easy. It requires patience, perseverance and a regular programme. But improving the quality of life and picking up again at the point where pain took over is not impossible.

The voice of another patient sums it up:

> 'I used to creak around a whole lot. Now I've got muscles that are working again. The pain is still there, but I can ignore it. I'm not aware of it and I think it's getting less. My life goes on as normal.'

By understanding more about your own pain and the potential within you to conquer it, you may be able to share this confidence.

How to Use This Book

Many people with chronic pain feel rather jaded, and may want to get straight on with the exercises, relaxation training and ways of coping that we outline. In that case, read Chapters 4, 5 and 6, and get started. Read Chapters 3, 7 and 10 to keep it going, and build up your knowledge about pain with the remaining chapters.

1

How pain works

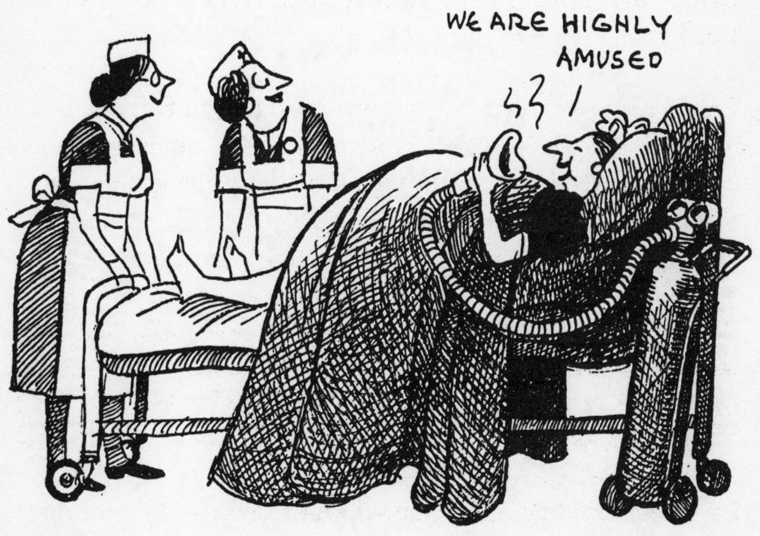

There was a time when bearing pain was thought of as something noble or character-building. From biblical times through to the Victorian era, withstanding pain was seen to be somehow admirable or meritorious. Happily, it was one Victorian attitude Queen Victoria herself did not share. Her subjects may have felt that there should have been no relief of labour pain but, when Victoria found herself pregnant, the old adage of 'in sorrow shalt thou bring forth children' went out of the window. The Queen pioneered anaesthesia *à la Reine* when she had pain relief during childbirth.

CHRONIC PAIN: A VICIOUS CIRCLE

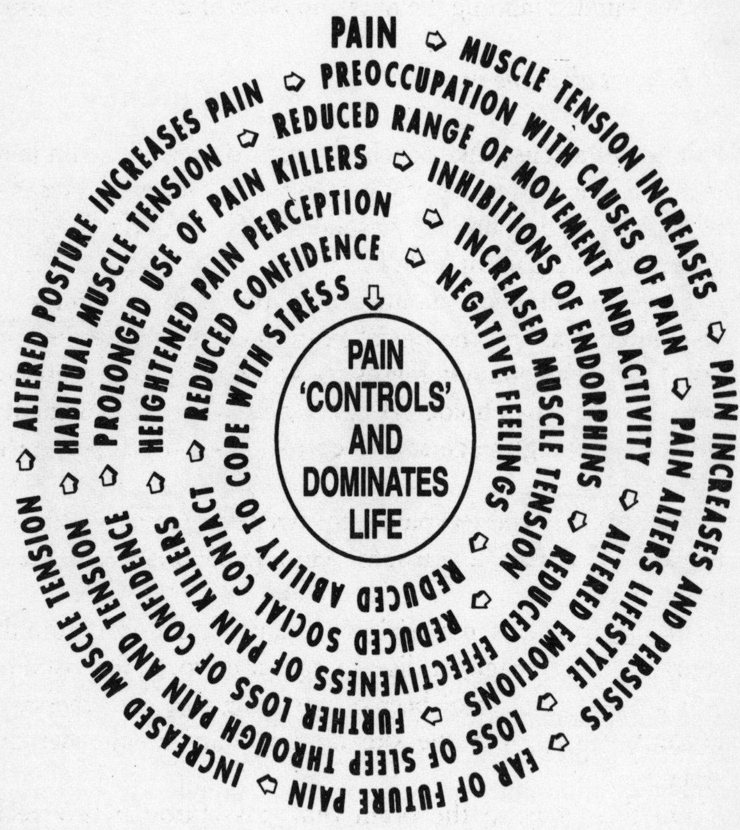

Her decision helped to outmode the idea that bearing pain is somehow heroic or necessary. We now know that long-term pain is negative and destructive and serves only to make us less of a person than we were previously. Fortunately, research in the last thirty years has disclosed much about the nature of pain. The first step towards releasing ourselves from pain involves understanding the nuts and bolts of how pain works.

But is it all in the mind?

Pain is not a sense, like touch, eyesight or hearing. Pain is an emotion. It is the reverse of pleasure and our language is rich in its imagery – 'it pains me to have to tell you', 'the pain of a broken heart', 'painful reality'.

People sometimes comment on the pain of others by dismissing it as 'psychological', by which they mean imaginary. This is one of many myths about pain. There is confusion here between psychological, or emotional, and imaginary. There is nothing imaginary or unreal about psychological or emotional pain.

The fact that you feel pain – for whatever reason – means it is real. So real that, if you suffer chronic pain, little else seems to matter.

Inside our bodies, pain follows a complex pathway from the source of the damage, or disease, to our brain. If, for instance, you drop a six-pack of beer on your big toe, pain messages instantly travel from the site of the injury up the nervous system.

On their way to the brain they pass through tiny relay stations at specific points. It is rather like calling London from New York City. You pick up the phone in your apartment and send messages which pass through a telephone exchange in New York. The exchange then transmits them across the Atlantic to another relay in London which, in turn, sends them to your friend's house. The clarity and sharpness of the messages depend on how the exchanges receive them and pass them on.

Similarly, there are two important relays in our nervous system that play a vital role in the intensity of pain we suffer. The pain message leaves our big toe and reaches the first relay station, situated in the spinal cord. There, it crosses over the midline of the spine and moves along another pain fibre – up the other side of the body – until it reaches the second relay in the subconscious brain. These relays are also known as pain gates. The pain message is then passed from there to the conscious brain, which evaluates the warning and reacts immediately.

The brain figures: 'There's a message coming in from the big toe nerve. There must be damage down there. Sound the alarm.' A millisecond later, we double up in pain and yell: 'Ouch!'

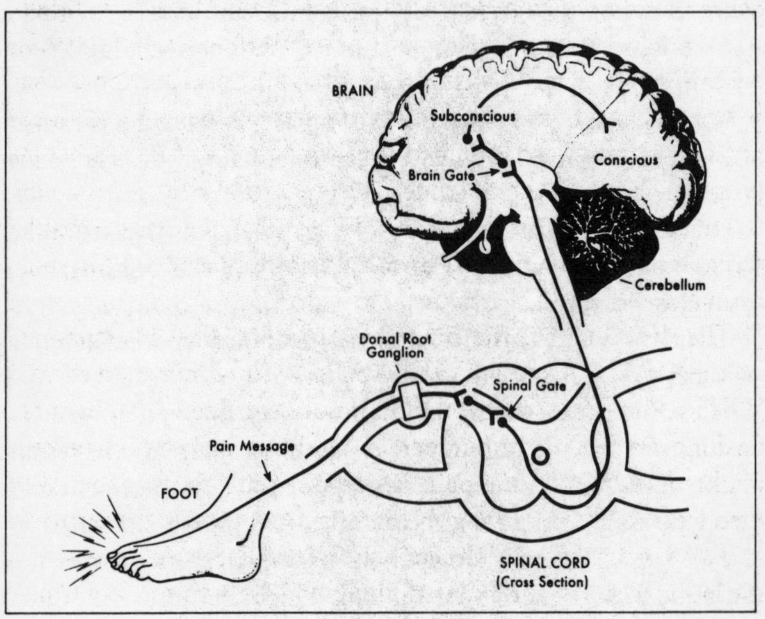

The important thing to appreciate about this is that the pain is experienced with the brain. When an anaesthetist puts you to sleep, he neutralizes the part of the brain that has the ability to feel pain. While the surgeon cuts through the skin and removes, say, a lump, and stimulates pain fibres in the process, the part of your body that receives the pain is inactive and therefore cannot feel it. The damage to the tissues is being done, the pain is being produced, but it has nowhere to register.

Similarly, if someone is severely brain damaged, the ability to feel pain is removed. This, in fact, is one of the recognized medical tests for 'brain death'. When a deeply unconscious person fails to respond to painful stimuli, it is a sign that the brain may be damaged beyond repair. Thus, no brain – no pain. We truly feel pain with our mind.

However, the brain has to tell us where the pain is coming from. It manages this by learning, over a period of time, which neves come back from particular areas of the body. The brain of a newborn baby is too immature to localize pain. If you stick a pin into a newborn baby, it rolls into a ball and screams. The baby is aware that something nasty has happened, but does not know where, so it pulls in all four limbs and assumes a protective posture. By the time the baby is one year old, if a pin is stuck into its left leg, the left leg moves and the baby screams. By this time it is aware that the pain is originating from a specific area.

The pain area of the brain works rather like a telephone switchboard, marked out in tiny lights with numbers on them. When the pain bell rings, the brain looks to see which light is flashing and what its number is. Number 123, for instance, might indicate that the pain is coming from the big toe. We then gasp 'ouch', knowing the pain is coming from the big toe.

This explanation is deceptively simple because, wherever the big toe nerve is stimulated along its six foot pathway from foot to brain, it will cause us to register and feel a pain in the big toe. Thus, if the big toe nerve is stimulated, say, behind the knee because it is pinched in some way, we get a pain down to our big toe. If the sciatic nerve is hit by a nurse's needle, we experience a pain shooting down the leg and into the big toe. If a slipped disc comes out and presses on the nerve root that runs back from the big toe then, accordingly, we feel pain in the big toe.

This is well-known to doctors. If you go to your GP complaining of severe pain shooting down the back of your leg into your big toe, which came on when you lifted something, it would be unlikely that he would make a thorough examination of your foot and toe and declare that nothing was wrong because your toe seemed all right. The doctor would immediately recognise this as a likely slipped disc and probably examine your back first. This kind of referred pain is no longer a mystery.

Even stimulation of the pathway in the brain will produce pain which appears to come back from the original commencement of the pathway. Curiously, the brain itself does not contain pain fibres of its own. The only pain fibres running through the brain come from other parts of the body. They run into specific sites, like motorways converging, and so a neurosurgeon can operate directly on the brain without causing pain. There are now special neurosurgical techniques which involve using local anaesthetics to numb the tissues and prepare a way down to the brain. Probes can then be inserted very accurately to locate one specific part of the brain. Once this has been done, an abnormally-functioning part of the brain can be treated.

On his way in to do this, the surgeon may just touch the pain track, which will produce an experience of pain, again perhaps going down the leg to the big toe if that particular branch of nerves is being stimulated. This pain is very real and also located in a specific area of the body, but the message that there is damage there is incorrect.

This explains what is known as phantom pain. If someone has their leg amputated, they may have lost twenty four inches of their body, but the remainder of the nerve that used to come from the amputated area still goes back up to the brain to represent that part of the body. Should that nerve become irritable at the time of the operation or afterwards – especially if it has been firing a lot before the operation – then the patient may experience a phantom limb and feel that his leg is still there.

Often, this is a painful sensation. In fact, some authorities estimate that more than half the people who have a leg amputated suffer phantom limb pain. Originally, people who had this condition tended not to talk about it. This is perhaps because many were soldiers wounded in battle. Admitting to feeling pain in a limb that had been removed was embarrassing and made others think that something was perhaps mentally wrong with them.

Gradually, amputees began to talk to each other and, realizing that the condition was quite widespread, were able to bring it to the attention of doctors. Although it was known for a long time that the phenomenon occurred, no one really understood why until the development of pain research in the 1960s.

Referred pain can often manifest itself in a heart attack, masquerading as severe pain in the arms, particularly the left arm. Patients arriving at the Casualty Department complaining of a severe pain in their left arm, looking pale and feeling slightly shocked would be suspected of having a heart attack, even though it is quite clear that their heart is not in their arm! The nerve supply from the heart and the nerves from the arm come from the same group of cells in the embryo. As the newborn baby generally never experiences cardiac pain in its learning process, we cannot always identify the pain from heart damage inside the chest. In a similar way, pain from the gall bladder is sometimes experienced behind the right shoulder, rather than in the stomach below the liver.

The importance of this is that when we say we have a pain and feel it in a specific part of the body, we may be right in that we have pain, but we may be very wrong in exactly where we believe the problem lies. Pain may often originate from a specific cause but, once the pain pathway has been open and operating for months or years, other factors come into play. Changes occur within the whole pain transmission process – circuits become hypersensitive and pain messages continue without the original stimulus.

This is the situation many chronic pain sufferers tend to find themselves in. Their original injury may be clearly understandable and would be expected to cause pain. Perhaps there was a torn muscle or ligament, nerve damage or a broken bone. Ten years later, when they attend the Pain Relief Clinic, the original cause has often settled down but the pain continues.

The patient, of course, feels that his pain is still coming from one specific part of his body, but when the doctor examines this area he can find nothing wrong. This can lead to misunderstanding between doctor and patient.

Like the transatlantic telephone call mentioned earlier, pain messages are a two-way traffic. Just as your friend in London reacts to what you say in New York, the brain responds by sending messages back again. Descending pain pathways reach from the brain down to the gates in the subconscious and the spinal cord.

The reason for this is that gates are places where the flow of pain messages can be controlled or influenced. By sending responses back, the brain can order the release of chemicals which actually reduce or inhibit pain sensations. These important pain-blocking chemicals, which we manufacture within our bodies, are called *endorphins*. They are the key to

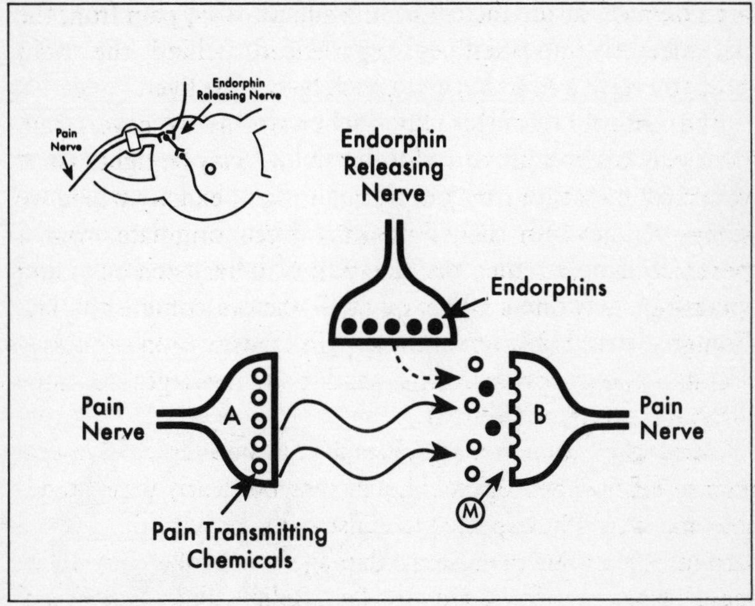

controlling pain and, with practice and patience, some people can learn how to release them at will. Endorphins – the body's own pain killers – are a powerful, natural weapon for reducing pain. Occasionally, we hear about them coming into use in times of extreme stress or shock: to help a wounded soldier keep moving on the battlefield; to enable someone to carry a child from a burning building; to help a sportsman with a broken ankle to finish his game.

If we were exposed to the full flow of pain at the time, we would be unable to function properly. In stress or danger, endorphins can block pain to give us time to escape and reach safety – an inbuilt ancient mechanism to ensure survival.

Research has shown that, as individuals, we seem to produce varying amounts of endorphins. Depending on how many we have in our system at any given time, they have a capacity to block pain a little, or a lot. Although endorphins are only one of the factors that influence the pain gates, they are extremely important.

If you have a head for mathematics, it works something like this: 1000 pain messages may start out from an injured toe on their way to the brain. If endorphins block 90 per cent of them, only 100 messages may get through the spinal cord gate. Of those, perhaps only ten will make it through to the conscious brain. In simple terms, the six-pack of beer you dropped on your foot generated 1000 'ouches' worth of pain, but your brain registered only ten of them.

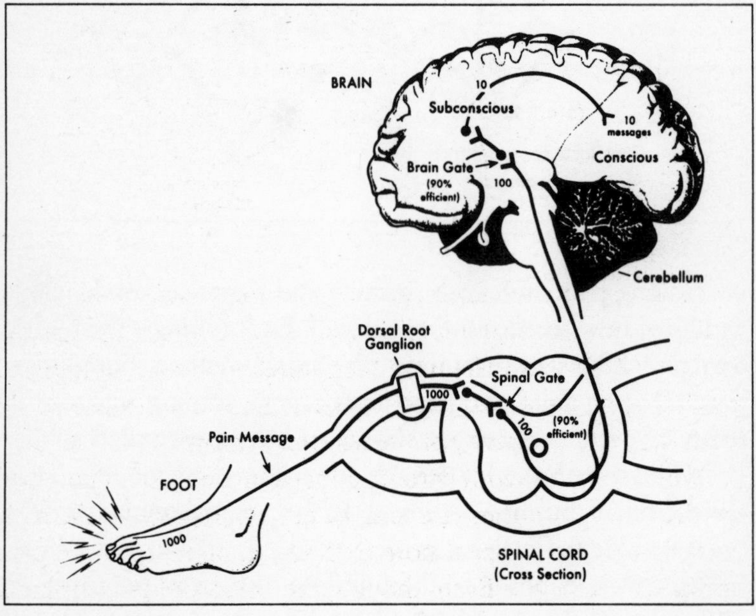

On another day, if the gates were only 50 per cent effective and you had the bad luck to drop another six-pack on the other foot when the gates were only working at half capacity, something different would happen. If the relays were only 50 per cent effective, 500 pain messages would pass up the spine and, of those, maybe 250 would reach the brain –that's 25 times worse than the previous accident.

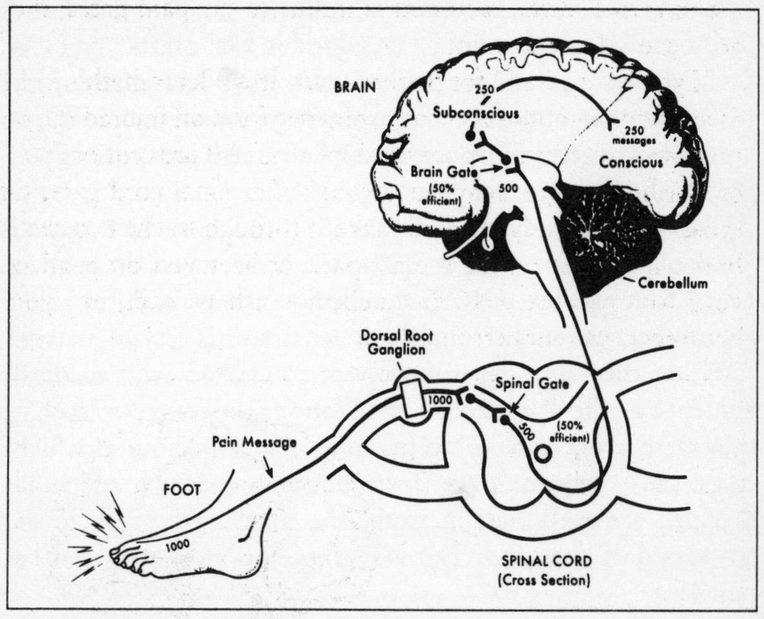

In effect you would have felt 25 times more pain, while suffering an identical injury to your toe. This tells us that the severity of what we feel is, in fact, unrelated to the amount of tissue damage we may have suffered and much more to do with the state of activity of the nervous system.

When someone with chronic, long-term pain feels depressed or despairing, or they are simply not coping too well, their relay station gates open more than usual, allowing more pain messages through. Even though the level of their original illness or injury remains the same, and the initial number of signals is constant, the pain itself increases. This also happens with many of the other psychological factors which influence pain. This interesting discovery dismissed the popular myth of 'pain thresholds'.

People watching a boxer in the ring may wonder how he has the capacity to take heavy punches. 'He doesn't seem to feel them,' they say. 'He must have a high pain threshold.'

Everyone, in fact, has more or less the same pain threshold. If someone is asked to hold a metal rod in a laboratory and it is then slowly heated or frozen until they feel discomfort, researchers can almost predict what those cut-off temperatures will be (43 degrees C for heat and −6 degrees C for cold, if you have a ghoulish interest in such things).

What varies from person to person is their *pain tolerance.* If we took the same people and asked them to try to bear as much pain as they possibly could, figures would differ enormously because our personal approach to pain is very important. When the same experiment was conducted with medical students at the Pain Relief Foundation, they were told that they were going to be subjected to terrible temperatures which could cause tissue damage. The students grimaced in pain and dropped the rods but, in truth, the machine was not even connected at the time. The very expectation of pain can be painful.

Pain tolerance not only differs from person to person but alters within the same person, according to circumstances and the way he or she feels. Experiments have been carried out to show, for example, that volunteers are prepared to tolerate more pain if friends or colleagues are watching, or even if a reward is offered. Many different factors regulate how much pain we can stand. An entertaining example is the Japanese game show where only contestants who tolerate extremes of pain and embarrassment go through to the next round and win a prize. Some fail miserably while others show amazing ability in controlling their discomfort.

The difference between our pain threshold, which we all share, and our individual pain tolerances is important because each relates to a quite different type of pain. When we trap our finger in a door, we go beyond our pain threshold. When we pass our pain tolerance – and pain becomes intolerable – we consult a doctor.

There are two types of pain – *fast pain* and *slow pain.* These can be likened to pricking your finger and pinching a thick fold of skin. The first triggers a fast pain message, while the second produces a slow, aching sensation.

The distinction can be noticed if you suddenly injure your toe. The first sensation is a sharp flash of pain, exactly at the point of contact. This gives way to a burning ache in the general area surrounding the injury. Because messages of fast and slow pain are quite different, they are carried from toe to brain along different kinds of pain pathway.

Fast pain – linked to our pain threshold – warns of sudden localized injury, so that the foot can be pulled away to avoid further damage. Slow pain, which is sometimes called deep pain, triggers a different reaction. Instead of jerking away in a reflex movement, the muscles often go rigid or contract, as though enforcing rest until the body can bring its natural healing into play.

The purpose of fast pain is to attract our attention – a sharp warning that we have been burned or pricked; that is to say, damaged in some way that requires a response to avoid further injury. Slow pain is a more complex emotional process, drawing on many kinds of information: memories of similar situations, how members of the family might have reacted in similar circumstances, or worrying if what we are feeling might lead to something worse.

Slow pain is linked to our pain tolerance which changes according to our past experience and our present state of mind. Our mental attitude can go a long way to influencing precisely how much slow pain we feel. Although these pains are very different, both can be helped by distraction: from the simple tactic of a mother rubbing her baby better when he has fallen over, to using hypnosis or music in the dental surgery to direct thoughts away from incoming pain messages.

Fast and slow pain messages are transmitted to the brain by pain *receptors* – a network of tiny nerve endings throughout the body which constantly monitor any sensations which might be out of the ordinary.

Fast pain receptors, *receivers* would be another way of describing them, are situated beneath the surface of the skin. Receptors for slow or deep pain share the same locations, but also carry messages from the joints and all the large internal organs of the body. These tiny sense organs pick up a variety of information to send to the brain: whether something is hot or cold to touch; whether something sharp or blunt is pressing against the skin. Some constantly feed back general information while others report damage or injury. Different receptors transmit different sensations so, for example, we can distinguish between the prick of a needle or a burn from a hot kettle.

It has been discovered that each type of pain receptor has its own individual pathway to carry messages to the brain. Morphine, for instance, can be used to block the slow messages of chronic pain, but has little effect on the fast pain messages caused by pricking your finger. Pain killers, in other words, work on our pain tolerance, but have little or no effect on our pain threshold.

The body allows us to cope with slow, chronic pain by using pain blockers such as morphine, or our own self-produced endorphins. It also provides a way of dealing with fast, reflex pain. By rubbing a knocked elbow, the amount of pain messages transmitted are cut down. The technique has been fine-tuned by medical science and doctors can achieve the same effect by electrical nerve stimulation, known as *TENS*, which is described in a later chapter. Vibration can also have similar benefits.

In simple terms, pain messages open the gates to flood through to the brain, while the action of rubbing closes the gates and cuts down the number of messages.

In recent years it has been found that messages are carried

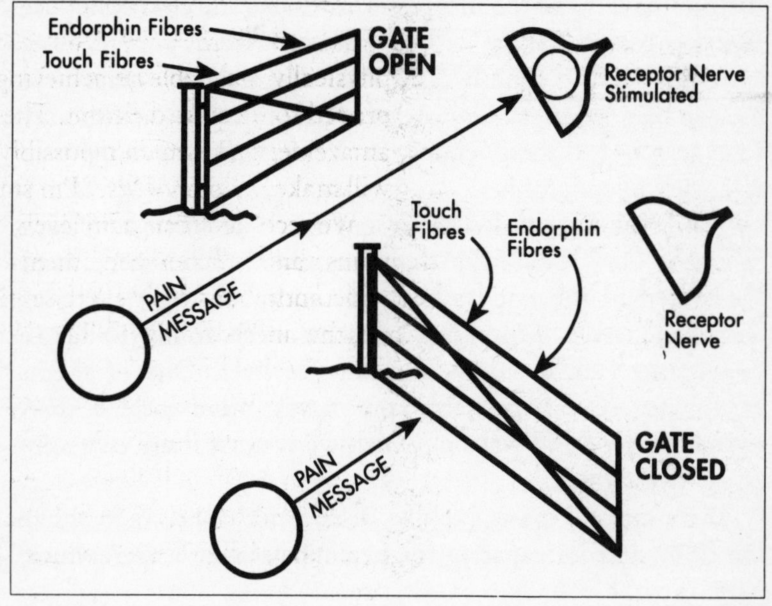

along pain pathways as an electrical current. One end of each cell has a receiver, which picks up the message, and the other contains a neural transmitter, a chemical substance, which passes it on by being released from one nerve ending and spreading to stimulate the next. Some pain killing drugs are designed to act on neurotransmitters and cut down the messages passing down the chain of cells.

Curiously, it was research into the pain killing properties of morphine that led to the discovery of endorphins. Morphine, derived from poppies, is probably the world's oldest pain killer – its use is shown by Egyptian hieroglyphics – but until the early 1970s, no one really understood how it worked. Morphine was found to enter the central nervous system and block the receptors of certain cells – like a key fitting a lock – to cut off pain.

What puzzled researchers was why the body had a lock

custom-made to fit the morphine key when the chances of the average person taking a drug derived from poppies was extremely slim. It soon became clear that the body must have its own pain killers, similar in molecular structure to morphine. The search for them ended in 1975 with the important discovery of endorphins.

The breakthrough led to an explosion of interest in pain research. One result was that compounds have since been discovered in the body which can stimulate the growth of damaged nerves. Morphine, too, has been found to break down into various compounds in the liver. One of them, Morphine 6G, is probably ten times more potent than morphine itself and ways in which we process it are currently being investigated.

There are still many exciting discoveries to be made about the body and its capacity for healing itself and overcoming pain.

Of course, all this information may seem to be of little value if, at this moment, you are suffering the agony of chronic pain yourself. In the long term, however, it is important to understand what is happening inside your body and to discover your potential for self-recovery.

Some pain persists for months, even years, forcing sufferers into social and financial hardship, aside from the damage to their emotional lives. Long-term pain has resisted every kind of conventional medicine for so many years that it is now recognized as the most common cause of disability in the United States. Nothing else causes the amount of misery, incapacity and suffering of chronic pain.

As we discovered in the introduction, *acute pain* is a warning which lasts only as long as the injury or disease. *Chronic pain* continues far beyond the normal process of healing.

If acute pain is not treated quickly and efficiently – or if the person is psychologically distressed at the time it arises – it can turn into chronic pain. The suffering of many patients can be avoided if the correct type of pain is diagnosed early and managed properly.

Research into pain relief is a relatively new science and discoveries are shared as widely as possible. An important step towards overcoming pain is for both sufferers and their family doctors to increase their knowledge of how pain works. With this understanding, the body's own healing mechanisms, which are safer and more enduring than drugs, can be harnessed and put to use.

Pain is not an illusion, but it is never quite what it seems. Research shows that *nociceptors* (nox-see-cep-tors) are nerve cells which transmit unpleasant impulses to the brain. The word, taken from 'noxious', refers to the number of pain nerve endings which are stimulated when an injury occurs.

Nociception, the transmission of pain impulses along various nerve fibre pathways to the brain, is not the same thing as pain itself. Along the way, embryo pain messages travel through the gates, or relay stations, we encountered earlier. Depending upon what is happening at these gates, messages become modified before finally emerging in the brain as a pain warning.

Pain, then, is a product of nociception, plus what is happening within the body and to our emotions at a given time.

Because pain tolerance varies according to emotional circumstances, a wounded soldier may feel less pain than someone run over by a bus. The soldier, who perhaps expected to be killed on the battlefield, would be delighted to find himself alive and relieved that he could feel anything at all. The unfortunate pedestrian who walked into the bus probably expected to spend the afternoon enjoying himself, without suffering any injuries at all. Their expectations were

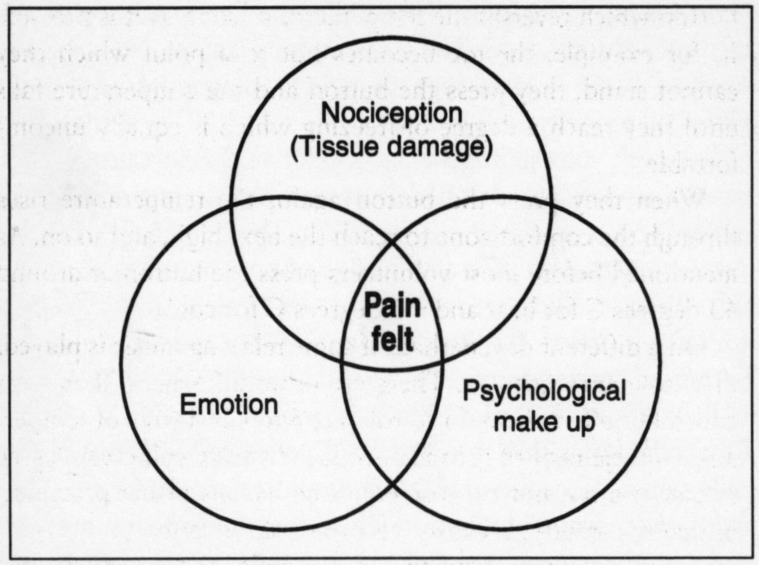

completely different and, thus, their pain is not comparable.

Pain tolerance is about the amount of pain we expect to receive and are prepared to put up with, depending upon how positive our outlook is.

Here, we have arrived at the whole purpose of this book: *Overcoming pain is a matter of learning how to control it.* Anyone who suffers chronic pain knows that being in charge of your own pain requires effort, energy and a positive outlook. It is far from easy to achieve because these are the very reservoirs of daily life that pain drains away. However, being in control can be achieved by learning how to manage yourself and by understanding what happens when pain takes over.

Volunteers who take part in pain tolerance experiments are good illustration of typical reactions to pain. Their responses provide an interesting mirror to hold up to yourself when you suffer pain. Each volunteer has a temperature probe attached to his or her big toe. Connected to the probe is a hand-held button which reverses the temperature as soon as it is pressed. If, for example, the toe becomes hot to a point which they cannot stand, they press the button and the temperature falls until they reach a degree of freezing which is equally uncomfortable.

When they press the button again, the temperature rises through the comfort zone to reach the next high, and so on. As mentioned before most volunteers press the button at around 43 degrees C for heat and −6 degrees C for cold.

On a different day, perhaps if some relaxing music is played, their tolerance goes up. There are other influences: if the test controller offers them £5 to tolerate another degree of temperature, an element of gain is introduced. Most volunteers agree to give it a try, not because everyone has his or her price but, more importantly, because every pain has its price.

If the volunteer happens to be male and a female test controller asks him if he can stand a few degrees more, the male pride lurking within will inevitably push him to agree. On the other hand, if both volunteer and tester are men, the tester might offer his subject an excuse for trying to be brave. 'You don't have to do this,' he says. 'I couldn't stand that much pain myself.' Once the volunteer has this assurance, he usually seizes the opportunity to duck out of the extra pain without losing face.

The button is important because it gives the volunteer control over the pain he experiences. In daily life, we are all equipped with similar personal buttons. The problem is that chronic pain pushes us so far out of control that we forget to use them.

On occasions, testers have secretly disconnected a volunteer's button to discover his reactions. When this vital control is removed, the temperature rises to the pain tolerance level and continues beyond it. The volunteer presses his button but, to his alarm, nothing happens. He jumps up yelling, as anyone would in the circumstances, and pulls the probe from his toe. He has not injured himself (testers are not in the torture business) but the pain was sharp enough not to entirely trust the experiment controller again.

When the tester apologizes and explains that wiring worked loose, reassuring him that it is securely plugged in again, human nature takes a hand. The experiment resumes but, this time, the volunteer presses his button to signal his tolerance level a good few degrees before he actually attains it. As soon as the heat sensation becomes even slightly uncomfortable, he immediately reverses the temperature.

There is an interesting lesson about ourselves contained here. The situation is similar to one everyone has experienced in the dentist's chair. The patient sits down and opens his mouth, knowing that the dentist is going to stick instruments into it and probe around. He knows that the dentist's next move will be to produce an enormous drill, which he does not like the idea of at all. At the first whine of the drill he stiffens in his chair and, when the dentist hits the tooth nerve, he possibly hits the roof.

The thought of being unable to tolerate pain has become a self-fulfilling prophesy. The patient suspected that his dental treatment was going to be unpleasant, and it was. In reality, half the problem lay in his apprehension, his lack of control and, finally, his embarrassment at screaming in front of the dentist and his nurse. His state of mind allowed many more messages than necessary through the pain gate.

The scenario, however, need not have proceeded like that. An understanding dentist might have said: 'Hold the nurse's hand and squeeze the moment you feel any pain. When that happens, I'll stop immediately. You won't feel any pain longer than a split second.'

The patient would have sat in the chair more relaxed and reassured. Although the dentist might be doing something which felt uncomfortable, he knew he had control over it. The difference meant that the patient could go right up to his tolerance level and stand the pain for several minutes, simply because of this control. This concept is important: how much pain you are prepared to tolerate depends upon the degree of control you have over it. You can learn how to control pain by being able to tolerate more of it so that the pain, in turn, becomes less unpleasant.

Many people in chronic pain find themselves out of control and desperately seek someone else to fix their pain for them. Their locus of control is poor. The more doctors they visit, the more hopeless and inadequate they feel as a patient. Eventually, they may find themselves at a pain clinic such as Walton Hospital where the first daunting words they hear from me may not be quite what they expected: 'We are not going to fix the pain for you, but we can teach you how to cope with it yourself.'

At this point, some patients lose interest before they have begun. They want to continue their search for the mythical 'right' doctor who will magically take away their pain for them. In the course of their quest, which may last a lifetime, they may encounter doctors who offer to operate, to prescribe new drugs for them, possibly even hit them on the head with a silver hammer if they are prepared to pay the fee.

All their valuable energy has been channelled into searching for someone to cure them, instead of utilizing that energy to help themselves. Because they have a poor, or external, locus of control, they are not interested in making an effort to cope without someone else offering to carry the burden. In effect, it becomes the sufferer's equivalent of the search by the Knights of the Round Table for the Holy Grail – a noble and understandable quest, but doomed to absolute failure because it did not exist.

The purpose of a pain management programme, and also

this book, is to help re-centre that lost locus of control and to work on being in control again. The results can be tremendously encouraging, both physically and mentally and in terms of restored confidence. Programmes also help to stimulate a positive outlook which is essential, not only for overcoming pain but for rebuilding a normal lifestyle again.

A great step towards doing the things you used to do is achieved through positive thinking – not a fanciful notion confined to 'How To Improve Yourself' books, but an important technique for training the mind to influence the body.

This is clearly illustrated in ulcer pain. Joe Matthews, a regional sales manager for a brewery, was a typical patient. He had been confined to hospital on a milk drip and had lost considerable time from work. After treatment, he was free from pain for six months and was about to go on holiday.

To clear a backlog of paperwork before his break, Joe had been burning the midnight oil and was suddenly struck by severe indigestion. His *emotional* reaction was one of panic. The only thought in Joe's mind was that his ulcer had flared again and another depressing period of illness loomed on the horizon. This was followed immediately by his *interpretational* reaction: 'My ulcer's back. I'll have to go into hospital. My holiday will have to be cancelled. Everything is ruined.'

Together, the two reactions caused so much stress that his stomach released excessive acid which, naturally, made the ulcer much worse. In short, another self-fulfilling prophesy.

By allowing his emotions to become worked up and by visualising a series of doom-laden events Joe, in effect, made them a reality. Psychologists call this *catastrophizing*, which is a perfect description. In a similar way, stress caused by negative thinking and catastrophizing by someone who has back pain can precipitate a muscle spasm which makes his whole condition worse.

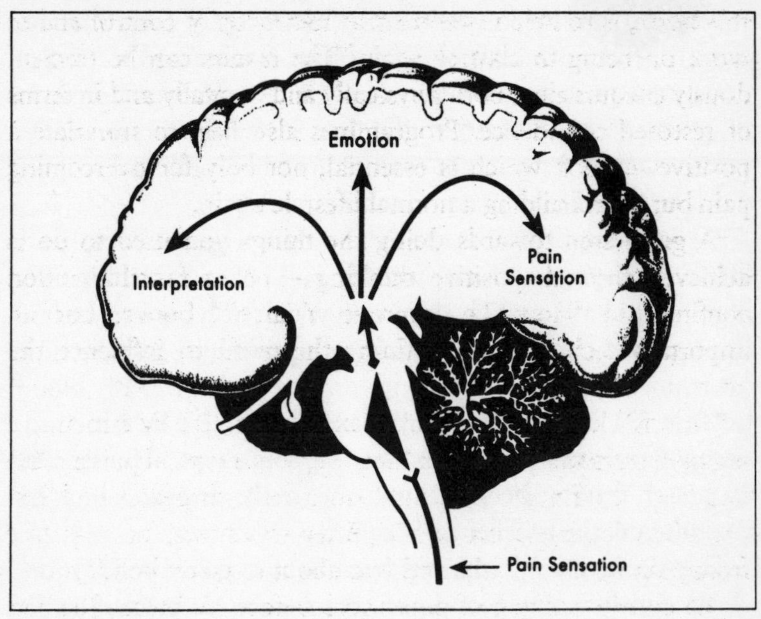

Logically, Joe need not have put himself through such double despair. If he had had a stronger locus of control, he might have taken a more positive approach to his ulcer – perhaps taking antacids, stopping smoking, adjusting his drinking habits and making a point of putting time aside each day to relax. His stomach would have secreted less acid and, by the time his holiday came around, it would probably have been well on the way to healing completely. Rather than miss his break, he could have returned home feeling refreshed and probably quite smug at his achievement.

Positive self-help, which would have resulted in a completely different pain scenario, requires more energy, effort, discipline and dedication. In the end, however, it would have paid off. Acquiring the habit of positive thinking, which we shall look at in depth later, also involves learning how to trick the body into drawing upon its own healing resources.

A similar approach was used by estate agent Tom Tarrant, who suffered from high blood pressure but learned a form of meditation to cope with the stress of city driving. If he was ploughing through heavy traffic, late for an appointment, the sight of a red traffic light was almost like pulling a trigger which sent his blood pressure soaring.

A positive approach made the red light trigger a completely different response. Tom would pull on his handbrake, delighted to have a whole minute in which to completely relax. The red light presented a wonderful opportunity to take time out from the hurly-burly of city driving and lower his blood pressure. By the time the light changed to green, he felt good, less anxious and fresh for his appointment. Unlike the harrassed drivers behind him, the more traffic lights he encountered, the happier he became.

This positive approach has been demonstrated to be more effective in lowering blood pressure than conventional medication. The problem is that when our physical and mental resources are low, summoning the effort to look after the body is very demanding. Like water seeking the lowest level, it is always much easier and requires less effort to reach for a tablet.

The temptation to place the problem of pain in someone else's hands is not really the easiest method at all. Joe's stomach ulcer, or Tom's high blood pressure, are symptoms of other things happening in life which usually result in stress. Like pain, they cannot be swept under the carpet by constantly relying on medication. When tablets are used to suppress symptoms, stress – like water forced through a leaky joint – will inevitably emerge in other ways until you find yourself on the familiar treadmill again.

Employing positive attitudes for the ulcer, and relaxation for blood pressure, makes you healthier in every sense. Not just physically and mentally, but by preventing further problems which might arise.

When you succumb to reaching for a tablet every time you feel ill, you never address the real issues which need to be resolved. The tablet may mask the symptoms but, beneath the illusion, you are still sick. Far from offering a solution which requires little effort, tablets often turn out to be a bitter pill to swallow.

When pain affects your emotional well-being, tablets are of little long-term help. The real solution lies on the reverse of the coin – a realization that your emotional and mental outlook can greatly affect the way you cope with pain.

2

Pain killer – or bitter pill?

Few people manage to go through life without turning for help to a pain killer. Chronic pain sufferers often taken them in quantity and it is easy to understand why. As pain becomes more difficult to cope with, reaching for medication to get through the day becomes an instinctive reaction.

It has been said that most of us suffer at least one twinge of pain a day for reasons that are never discovered. Judging by the vast range of remedies on chemists' shelves, anyone would be forgiven for thinking that most people are in pain all the time. Pain killers are now so commonplace that we take them without thinking. But, just as we need to understand why we are in pain and how pain works, it is equally important to know something about the tablets we take.

Are they doing their job? Are they the right tablets for your particular condition? How long should you take them for? Indeed, should you be taking them at all?

The longer you have chronic pain, the more stubbornly it refuses to go away and, in turn, forces the sufferer to search for stronger medications to control it. Drug treatment for pain is referred to by doctors and pharmacists as the *analgesic ladder.* Most pain killers fall into three groups: aspirin, codeine or morphine. Chronic pain patients are progressed up the ladder by their GP's when the pain worsens and they can find no other relief.

If you have pain at this moment and are using over-the-counter remedies, or drugs prescribed by your doctor, they will probably be medications on one of the three rungs of the analgesic ladder (see Appendix on page 228).

Over-the-counter drugs are usually step one, or aspirin-like; codeine and morphine are controlled substances because they can be abused. Some over-the-counter remedies have a very slight amount of codeine in them, but the amount is so small that it probably has no clinical effect. Fortunately, drugs prescribed by your doctor are usually in the first or second category. As we will see later, it is very undesirable to give morphine-like drugs for chronic pain, except for cancer.

Patients who move up the ladder seeking relief find that some drugs have greater or lesser effect on their pain and, in doing so, make physical and mental demands of them. The initial optimism at embarking on a new course of drug treatment often distracts people from considering the side effects which may follow.

Even the aspirin group, the mildest tablets on the lowest rung of the ladder, can have unexpected side effects. Perhaps more than any other type of medication, people take these simple analgesics by trusting their chemist's advice, without any basic understanding of them. The pain killers they buy may be entirely inappropriate for their condition.

Patients with migraine, for example, have arrived at the Pain Clinic seeking relief and have been found to be taking indomethacin, a pain killer which can actually cause headache. A typical case was that of Annie, a Leicester housewife who found herself almost incapable of functioning because of intense headaches. She was taken off indomethacin and recovered with little further treatment.

This, of course, is not to say that simple pain killers are ineffective or bad for you. Many are the result of sophisticated pharmaceutical research – and perhaps even more sophisticated marketing. They have an excellent effect in relieving minor pains which do not require a visit to the doctor. It is a question of tailoring the particular product to your type of pain. Keeping a supply of simple analgesics handy is sensible self-management, but they should be a type which you know from experience do not upset you.

We tend to chose a particular brand of simple analgesic from habit, often conditioned by what we were given during childhood, or what we are most familiar with. Chemists' shelves are stacked with them, but none has ever consistently been proved best. Over-the-counter treatments usually contain aspirin, ibuprofen or paracetamol. Quite often, you find them in combination with other substances, but this does not normally offer any particular advantage.

The aspirin-like group, including aspirin and ibuprofen, are known as *Non-steroidal Anti-Inflammatory Drugs* (NSAIDs).

Or, as one of my colleagues, Dr Jesmond Birkhan, cynically puts it: A New Sort of Aspirin In Disguise.

Damaged tissues release prostaglandins, hormones which irritate nerve endings and help nerve fibres carry pain messages to the brain. Generally, over-the-counter remedies inhibit production of prostaglandins, and so reduce inflammation and pain. NSAIDs are sold by your local chemist in smaller doses than those prescribed by your GP. Recent evidence, however, suggests that some of the side effects of NSAIDs, which include the worsening of even mild cases of kidney disease, can occur at these lower doses.

Aspirin, common to most simple analgesics, is sold everywhere because so many people have become used to it. It is, however, a potent drug with significant side effects and many of the alternatives are, in fact, safer. Paracetamol, in particular, is milder with fewer worrying side effects.

Aspirin can be taken quite safely but, in some people, it may cause nausea, indigestion, dizziness or ringing in the ears. It has been estimated that one quarter of people who take aspirin get some bleeding in the gastro-intestinal tract; and that one quarter of people admitted to hospital with severe internal bleeding have taken aspirin in the previous 24 hours.

If you experience any bleeding, asthma, skin rashes or confusion, stop taking it immediately and see a doctor. Prolonged use may also cause liver or kidney damage.

Unless the circumstances are exceptional, it should never be used by people with a history of stomach ulcers, bleeding problems, severe indigestion, asthma, liver or kidney disease, severe allergies, pregnancy, lactating mothers or children under 12. In the case of teenagers, evidence suggests that aspirin may be a factor in Reye's Syndrome, a rare but serious form of liver failure.

It is almost certain that, if aspirin were a new drug being released today, it would never be allowed on medical prescription by a doctor because of the relatively high incidence of side effects. Ironically, however, there would probably be an outcry if attempts were made to remove it from chemists' shelves.

Paracetamol, in comparison, is safe to use during pregnancy and the side effects are rare. The mildest are skin rashes and allergies and the worst liver or kidney damage, but only in cases of overdose. It is therefore essential *never* to take more than the prescribed dose, particularly as doing so does not actually produce any extra pain relief.

If you are in any doubt as to what type of medication you have been given, ask your doctor or consult the drugs list at the back of the book.

There are some basic rules of thumb for using over-the-counter medications safely:

- Aside from the obvious precautions of following the instructions and not exceeding the dosage, it is important to read carefully what the medicine contains. Someone allergic to asprin, for example, may need to avoid other over-the-counter medications which contain asprin-like ingredients, such as magnesium salicylate, carbasprin calcium, choline salicyate and sodium salicylate.

- Unless your GP says otherwise, you should impose a cut-off period of ten days for over-the-counter painkillers. Children and teenagers should take them for no longer than five consecutive days. For all ages, tablets should never be taken more than three days when there is fever.

- Similarly, don't take asprin in the final three months of pregnancy, unless your doctor recommends it, as asprin can cause bleading in both mother and child.

- **Reye's Syndrome is rare but potentially fatal. Children and teenagers should not take asprin for chicken pox, flu or flu-like symptoms. No one under 14 should take asprin at all without specific instructions from their doctor.**

- **Don't take asprin for several weeks before surgery unless your doctor specifically recommends its use.**

As the vast majority of drugs on the analgesic ladder are likely to be prescribed by your GP, it is important to use your family doctor as effectively as possible.The more you complain about pain, the more he will be likely to prescribe stronger drugs, so there are questions you should ask.

- **Are these tablets addictive?**
- **What side effects do they have?**
- **Is it advisable to take them long term?**
- **Is there a tablet I can take less often?**

The second rung of the analgesic ladder has codeine-like drugs, and the third rung has morphine-like drugs. Obviously morphine is an addictive drug, and whilst it is excellent for acute pain such as post-operative pain or heart attacks, and also some cases of cancer pain, it cannot be used for chronic pain, as a general rule. The danger is that the effect will wear off, and the sufferer will need more and more morphine to gain the same relief. A state of addiction will gradually be reached, and some of the pain the sufferer then feels when it is time for the next dose might be part of a mini-withdrawal phase, rather than anything to do with the original problem. Whilst this is widely recognized by most doctors, the same cannot be said about codeine. However, when codeine-like drugs, including dihydrocodeine, distalgesics, DF118s and dextro-propoxyphene are given for more than 6 months, the same thing can occur. This is when it is especially important to ask the doctor about the possible addictive nature of the drugs, and if it is reasonable to take them long-term.

There are also questions you should ask yourself. If you regularly take drugs for chronic pain, you may understandably want to cut down on them. Firstly, are they doing their job? More specifically – can you function normally while taking them?

A well-known barrister who was a patient suffered severe pain and regularly took a drug on the codeine rung of the analgesic ladder. He was concerned that it might not be suitable for him. In conversation, it emerged that not only could he work in court without problems but, at weekends, he played polo or went fell-walking in the Lake District.

He was advised to continue with his medication. The barrister functioned normally on his particular drug and clearly would not have been as able to cope as well without it.

Other chronic pain patients have painted a different picture when asked about their daily activities. Some watch TV all day or, at most, manage to sit and knit.

Their problem is that they have become dependent on medication which suppresses some of the pain, but not all of it. They are hardly doing anything because the drug is also suppressing their will and a normal desire to be active. The medication is not only ineffective in doing its job, but having a profoundly negative effect on their physical and mental well-being.

An extreme example of this, relating to morphines, occurred in the days when the British provided opium dens for Chinese peasants. After a hard day's work, the peasants collected just enough money to obtain a pipe of opium to sustain their habit overnight. In the morning, they had to go to work to take their mind off withdrawal symptoms and to earn enough for the next night's supply. The idea was to subjugate them by providing only enough money for the next pipe of opium.

Many pain killing drugs demand a price from the patients who need them to get through each day. The help they offer is on a scale of diminishing returns. The more you rely on them, the less effective they become at suppressing pain – and the greater demands they impose mentally and physically. Relying entirely on tablets to relieve pain means that any gain you expected is overshadowed by demands the drugs make. Progress slows to nil – both in daily life and in overcoming pain.

Alongside the analgesic ladder are drugs known as *secondary analgesics.* These are tablets which usually have another prime purpose in life, but doctors have discovered that one of their spin-off effects is to reduce certain types of pain. The most important of these are drugs which affect the central nervous system in some way so, as well as their primary purpose, they will modify pain. These include tranquillizers, anti-convulsants and anti-depressants.

Many patients are prescribed tablets for pain relief without realising that they may be taking a tranquillizer, such as a benzodiazepine. These include diazepam (Valium) and lorazepam (Ativan), a newer drug which was thought to be less addictive but, in fact, is actually more addictive. Chlordiazepoxide was used for years and initially thought to be totally safe, but many patients are still chronically addicted. The drug is now rarely prescribed to new patients. Equagesic is a combination of tranquillizer and aspirin. There is a variety of common names or trade names for these drugs, Valium being perhaps the most well-known.

The purpose of the particular family of secondary analgesics is to work as a muscle relaxant, especially in cases of back pain. They are also addictive if taken regularly. Quite often, patients who take them have no idea that they are on Valium. In different circumstances, they would probably even refuse to take drugs of this type.

Patients preoccupied with chronic pain may not realize that it is unwise to take this group of drugs for longer than six weeks. At the end of that period they should be discontinued, otherwise the tablets take over the function of the muscles. Someone suffering from, say, back pain caused by muscle spasms, may discover that their muscles are unable to relax of their own accord again without depending on the tablets.

The result is that they no longer have control over their muscle spasm, because the work has been left entirely to the tablets. They become locked into a cycle of chronic pain. It is important that any of the benzodiazepine family of secondary analgesics should be regarded as short-term drugs. When they are taken for longer periods, patients become physically and mentally dependent for the temporary sense of relief and euphoria.

Another group of secondary analgesics is the *anti-convulsants*, normally used to treat epilepsy. Chronic pain is not normally associated with epilepsy, but the ability of these drugs to stabilize nerve membranes may be the reason they benefit some people.

They work in this way on epilepsy by stopping the hyper-irritability which produces messages going down to the muscles to make them twitch. In chronic pain, they work by reducing excessive electrical activity, within the spinal cord and brain, that brings pain messages back up to the brain. They have proved particularly useful in providing pain relief for shooting pain or knife-like stabbing pain.

These are pains which involve nerve irritation or nerve damage, such as post-shingles neuralgia, diabetic neuropathy or the almost unbearable pain of trigeminal neuralgia. They can be so severe that they completely change the sufferer's personality and lifestyle.

A patient called Sydney was known in his Cheshire village as an eccentric recluse. On the few occasions he ventured out, he had an unkempt beard and his coat collar pulled high over his head, even on the hottest day. He looked suspicious and deranged and his face was pale and gaunt.

Unknown to his neighbours, Sidney was a victim of extreme pain – in his case trigeminal neuralgia – which makes the face so sensitive that eating, shaving, talking, or even exposure to the slightest breeze can cause agony. Sydney rarely ate because it hurt to eat; he seldom talked because talking was painful. He hardly ever went out and had no one to help him. When he arrived at the clinic, he was a lonely, frightened man and a total prisoner of his pain.

He was offered anti-convulsant tablets used for treating epilepsy. On his next visit there was a remarkable transformation. For the first time in years his collar was folded down, his manner was more confident and his neuralgic pain was noticeably more under control. Sydney eventually went on to have a simple nerve block operation to complete his treatment and his life changed completely. (Further information of the treatment of trigeminal neuralgia can be found in Chapter 8.)

The lesson here is that tablets are useful tools of treatment if taken wisely and effectively.

Even so, anti-convulsants may have side effects with long term use. Patients can become unsteady on their feet and prone to blood disorders. Some may have to take anti-convulsants for years but, with careful monitoring and reduced doseages when necessary, the unpleasant effects of the drug can be controlled.

Other commonly-prescribed secondary analgesics are the anti-depressants. Anti-depressants are not addictive and can be used for long periods, particularly for peripheral nerve damage, such as shingles or the 'burning foot' sensation of diabetes. They are thought to help by interfering with serotonin and noradrenalin, chemical transmitters of nerve impulses.

They can be used when there is no depression, although mild depression often accompanies chronic pain. But they can have uncomfortable side effects, such as fatigue and bladder-emptying problems.

One of the benefits of anti-depressants is that they are only taken at night and tend to help chronic pain sufferers to sleep restfully. The pain may be just as bad during the day, but a welcome opportunity to sleep helps them cope better.

One of the problems facing patients in Britain is that information about the effects of the drugs they are prescribed is withheld from them. Even doctors are not always given the full facts they need to assess a new drug and sales campaigns can often be misleading.

In 1991, a report by the National Consumer Council called for wider information on the side effects of drugs. 'Patients are encouraged to trust unquestionably in the medicines they are prescribed,' the report concluded. 'When things go wrong, they find the system effectively abandons them, usually with no explanation, no apology and no hint of what might be done to redress the situation.'

The tests drugs have to pass in Britain are classified secret and the Department of Health would break the law if it revealed a particular drug's ingredients. To complicate matters, patients are not always told if a drug has been withdrawn. In the chain of information, the pain sufferer is generally considered last.

'The consumer is like the person at the end of the line in Chinese Whispers,' Lady Wilcox, Chairwoman of the N.C.C. commented. 'In between is a vast chain of decision-makers; manufacturers, government and regulatory committees, NHS policy makers and managers, GPs, hospital doctors and pharmacists.

'They often give the impression that the person actually

taking the medicine is best kept in the dark. It is time consumers had more say in the regulation and control of prescription medicines.'

Secondary analgesics can be an enormous help to patients. Ken Hurst, a warehouseman, struggled to hold down his job while suffering chronic back pain. His family doctor prescribed codeine, which did not help at all. At the Pain Clinic, he was prescribed Amitriptyline, 50 mg at night, which greatly relieved the problem.

What may have suited Ken, however, may not be appropriate for the next patient to come along. Response to drugs varies from person to person. It is important to take a balanced view of what your tablets are actually doing to help cut down pain. You should not take steps to reduce them simply because you don't like the idea of taking drugs. If they are generally working to reduce pain and allow you to lead a normal life, there is no reason to stop taking them.

Many tablets, however, do not have these ideal properties. Drugs on the codeine and morphine rungs of the analgesic ladder, for example, tend to suppress the body's natural ability to inhibit pain. It is not fully understood why this occurs, but it would not be unreasonable to imagine that drugs like morphine subjugate the body's own pain-reducing mechanism by inhibiting the production of endorphins.

If we see the body as full of tiny endorphin-producing factories, turning out substances to combat pain, and the 'market' is suddenly flooded with morphine, it would be natural for them to go out of business. When morphine provides pain inhibitors of similar molecular shape, the body's own endorphin factories shut down.

When the time comes to reopen, they may be in no fit state to do this and may be unable to produce endorphins. Consequently, the patient will suffer out of all proportion to the physical disease.

The key to long-term pain control lies within yourself, rather than a doctor who may prescribe drugs or surgery. For someone suffering chronic pain, this is not an easy concept to grasp, because pain has a habit of altering your perception, attitude and general outlook. If you can't think straight, it is difficult to put your pain in perspective.

The first steps to overcome this lie in realizing that *the severity of pain is not related to the severity of illness.* Anyone can die just as easily from a painless heart attack as a painful one. Some forms of cancer, particularly the leukaemias, can be quite malignant without being painful at all. Other types of cancer are extremely painful, but this has no bearing on their toxicity.

Changing your attitude to pain by placing it in perspective has a great effect on how much pain you can tolerate without it interfering with normal daily life.

Most hospital casualty staff know that some people wheeled in with horrific injuries do not seem to be in much discomfort, whilst someone with a minor sprain might be in agony. Similarly, some of those patients with minor sprains causing intense pain may find it has disappeared by the time they reach the casualty department. Again, someone else with a sprain might feel no pain, yet be screaming by the time he arrives at hospital.

Obviously, there is a principle here worth considering. The injury or illness may be the same, but the pain does not relate to its severity. In other words, *pain is often out of all proportion to disease.*

Changing your attitude to pain is not as easy as it may sound. Coping with pain is something we unconsciously learn as children and are conditioned by as we grow up. How we learn to tolerate pain is so deep-rooted that it varies from person to person, family to family and even country to country.

One study of cultural differences was made in a World War

Two hospital for the wounded. Soldiers from Jewish–American and Italian–American backgrounds, for example, expressed their pain more emotionally than Irish–Americans and 'Old Americans'.

There are also differences between the sexes. Boys, for instance, are taught that they are expected to cope with pain, while girls learn that there is not the same pressure on them to bear pain without crying. Traditionally, boys are expected to play rugby – a game in which getting hurt is common – without running to the side-line every time someone knocks them over. Girls, on the other hand, are not expected to indulge in such aggressive pastimes. These observations are not meant to be sexist. They are established patterns of how children are brought up in today's society.

One result of this conditioning is that the Walton Pain Programme treats three times more women than men. The important point, however, is that within these numbers certain people will cope differently to others. Introverts, extroverts, people who are naturally relaxed and those generally tense all possess traits which regulate how much pain they experience and complain of.

People who suffer physical and sexual abuse as a child are more likely to suffer chronic pain than the general population. If this is true in your case, you should seek help from a trained counsellor or psychologist, through your doctor.

Once patients begin to talk about themselves, family histories of pain are often uncovered. If, for example, a child had a parent who suffered from chronic pain and could not cope very well with it, then there is a strong chance that the child will not learn to cope with pain, either. Alternatively, someone who had a parent who was ill, but rarely made the family aware of it, would possibly grow up to become good at coping themselves.

The classic, and most bizarre case of coping skills, was the ancient Spartans who were punished as children if they showed pain. When they grew up and became soldiers, this gave them something of an advantage. If a Spartan was severely wounded in battle, he was often able to ignore the pain of his wounds and continue to fight on.

Of course, this is an extreme example. The fact remains that we are conditioned as children and the amount of pain we experience has a direct bearing on the spinal gates which control pain. A person who is able to cope well will have gates which are fairly well closed and allow through only a small amount of pain. A less experienced coper will suffer more pain.

Conditioning of this kind is hard to undo, but you can make progress towards it by trying to put your pain in perspective. Most acute pain warns of tissue damage. When a caveman woke up to find a sabre-tooth tiger gnawing his leg, the pain message would instantly tell him to run as fast as he could. It warned him that he needed an acute reaction to the life-threatening situation he found himself in. His attitude to pain, putting it mildly, would be a major response. Pain would be the most vital thing he was feeling and his brain would rate it as the most important sensation.

This rulebook does not apply to chronic pain. If someone has had a painfully arthritic knee for years then the pain, in some ways, is not particularly important any more. The sufferer can argue with his subconscious: 'The pain this morning does not mean that there is any new disease in my knee. It was hurting years ago and will probably continue to hurt in the future. I can safely ignore the pain because it is no different to the way it has ever been.'

Your attitude to pain, therefore, should not be that it is something enormous and terrible because you have suffered so long. By changing your perspective and rationalizing what you feel, you can tell yourself: 'If the pain has been there for that length of time, perhaps I don't need to take so much notice of it.'

In chronic pain cases there is rarely any ongoing disease process to worry about, yet patients locked into their pain often fear the opposite. They feel that the longer their pain persists, or the worse it becomes, the more their illness is progressing and taking hold of them.

Pain and illness are two separate entities. Once you convince yourself of that, you are half way to changing your attitude towards pain. If your pain happens to be particularly bad today, try to place it in perspective. Some days may be good and others unbearable, but it does not mean that you are more ill and your health is deteriorating.

Occasionally, the situation may be made worse by a GP who feels unable to cope with a particular patient. He may examine someone's back and say without thinking: 'You've got the spine of a 90-year old.' The patient goes home negatively brooding over every word, forgetting that some 90-year olds live a completely normal life.

The fact is that family doctors and orthopaedic surgeons sometimes find themselves challenged by long-term pain sufferers. The patient looks to them hopefully for recovery but, in many cases, therapeutic treatment is impossible. The surgeon may scrutinise the X-rays, shake his head and remark: 'Your back is in a terrible state. I'm sorry, but there's nothing I can do for you. It's beyond repair.' Doctors, after all, are in the business of making people well. They may feel inadequate dealing with long-term cases where tablets have little effect and chances of recovery are slim.

Chronic pain patients may leave a consultation feeling badly treated, but the doctor may also have his own problems. When he treats patients he expects their condition to improve. If, for visit after visit, a chronic pain sufferer fails to respond, the doctor may have difficulty coping, too. In the back of his mind is a waiting room full of patients whom he probably has a reasonable chance of curing.

Subconsciously, he may think that if he can dispense with the 'incurable' long-term sufferer and move on to more easily-treated cases, he will feel more fulfilled. The doctor may rationalize his frustration by bluntly telling the patient just how bad his condition is, in the hope that he will go away and try to come to terms with it. That way, no one can blame the doctor for his failure to 'cure'.

Unfortunately, this negative approach seldom works in practice. While it is true that some patients desperately want a diagnosis, once they have been baldly informed of the facts, they feel unable to cope. After badgering the doctor to be honest, they mull over his diagnosis and conclude that it would have been better never to have known they had an arthritic spine. The prospect of being crippled for life proves to be too much to bear.

If, instead, the surgeon had commented: 'Your back has had more than the average wear and tear. But it's no worse than similar cases I've seen. I certainly don't think you need surgery,' then the patient's attitude might have been completely different.

Professional footballers and rugby players quite often have damaged spines, but still turn out to play every weekend. There is no question that they are in pain, but they do not allow it to affect their performance. People should evaluate their pain – even to the point of obtaining a second opinion – and find out if there is any reason why they should not be more mobile.

Obviously, if you have a fractured leg you should not walk on it and make it worse. However, if you have a bad back and indulge in some activity which makes it hurt the next day, this does not mean that you have damaged yourself. It more likely indicates that you are unfit. The way to overcome this is to achieve modest targets until, with practice, you can get around with less discomfort.

The importance of targetting, as we shall see, is never to lower your expectations because of fear of hurting yourself. Occasionally, there have been patients on the Pain Management Programme who have had post-exercise pain the day after doing their T'ai Chi exercises and have complained to their GP of stiffness and discomfort. The doctor, who understandably had more pressing matters to attend to, advised them to stop exercising if it hurt!

What the patients failed to understand was that, subconsciously, they were engineering a situation which would allow them to stop exercising. If they had asked, more reasonably, 'Is it harming me to have this pain?' it is probable that their doctor would have thought not and have advised them to go on.

Providing your doctor says it is safe for you to take gentle exercise, you should adopt a positive attitude, believing that it will improve your ability to cope with pain.

At the Pain Research Foundation we asked people with lower back pain if they would help with a survey to measure pain-controlling endorphins which are released into the bloodstream with exercise. The idea was to monitor their blood levels before and after exercise to identify the endorphins they produced.

Before we began, we worked out what level of exercise we thought they would be capable of, by using Swedish averages. The Swedes, a gymnastically-inclined nation, calculate that a 60-year-old man, for example, should theoretically be able to pedal so many minutes up a hill with an incline of so many degrees.

We made a realistic guess that the British would be less fit than cycling Swedes and took only two-thirds of their figures as a base. Then, because we were dealing with pain patients, we reduced the target by half. So we ended with an over-safe estimate of about a third of what our patients should have been able to accomplish on the exercise machines.

This was our volunteers' target and none of them were physically incapable of achieving it. Their attitudes, however, proved to be quite different. The general consensus was one of amazement. 'I couldn't possibly do that,' they protested. 'It will make my pain worse. I'm simply not capable of it.'

We recorded their pain levels, took blood to measure endorphins and encouraged them to try. They climbed very reluctantly onto their exercise bikes to pedal for a fixed time, on the understanding that they could stop whenever they wanted to.

When the results were collected, most had stopped well below the target they had been set, which was quite low to begin with. Instead of exercising for ten minutes, they had mentally set themselves a goal of three minutes and achieved five. Their pain scores, which were measured later, had not risen.

The patients were proud of their achievement because they all believed they had attained good results. They had all stopped, not because their pain had worsened, but because they thought it was unwise to do more in case it was 'bad' for them.

Naturally, the test had been set up so they could not possibly harm themselves, but they were so afraid that they pulled up well within a safety margin of their own invention. Their attitude towards themselves was that they did not think they were capable of ten minutes' exercise. When a demand was made on them, they quickly rationalised, decided to achieve less and were finally delighted because they scored higher than they thought possible.

What really happened was that their constant lowering of goals prevented them from achieving their potential. They applied a mental brake to something they were easily capable of – then congratulated themselves on being such a success!

Pain, in other words, changes our attitude. It forces the sufferer to forget that he was once a positive person and, like water, to always seek the lowest level; to err on the side of caution and always compromise, to constantly seek out the negative until he becomes less of a person than he was before.

This need not be so. Experience shows that patients who determinedly work to change their attitude, and make a positive effort to do more, discover that their tolerance to pain improves. The farewell speech given by one patient, Barbara, at the end of her four-week Pain Management Programme, illustrates her improvement. She joined the course after suffering chronic back pain in a car accident in 1989:

> 'After the usual carousel of GP, hospital, consultant, GP, hospital, pain killer, operations and injections, I was bluntly told that nothing could be done for my injury and pain. I felt very angry. I had lost my job, my hobbies, my social life. I was at war with the world and my family.
>
> 'I could hardly do a thing for myself, the pain in my back was so bad. I was also very stiff – all my back muscles were in spasm and I had no control over them. Through this period my GP, family and friends were very supportive. They stopped me from going into deep depression.
>
> 'I am not a loser and would not accept the fact that this situation was to be my life. I was 42 years old and had no intention of going through life pill popping. I didn't care what it took – I was determined to have myself a normal life again. When my GP suggested the Walton Pain clinic, I was ready to try anything.
>
> 'At my appointment, Dr Wells told me that I must be prepared for four weeks hard work, and that would be just the tip of the iceberg. He said he could not cure my pain, but he could give me a better quality of life. I was desperate. I was prepared to try anything and give it 101 per cent.

'Deep inside I was scared and very apprehensive and fearful of doing myself more damage.

'I attended the clinic not knowing what to expect and was introduced to the team and the programme. Everyone was so helpful, so understanding. People cared. Everyone wanted me to do well and nothing was too much trouble. Even the other people on the course, who were in pain themselves, encouraged me. I felt that there was light at the end of the tunnel. At last I was coming out of the labyrinth of darkness.

'I found the exercises very painful and at one time I thought I was going to die, but I worked even harder. The relaxation helped me find a way through the pain and my negative thoughts. At last, my body was doing what I wanted it to do, not what the pain wanted. Once I realized that hurt did not mean harm, I really pushed myself.

'I began to realise that self-discipline and self-control were a necessity. Slowly, the fear and the anger started to fade. These two emotions would pull me back if I didn't let go. I learned, not just to rest, but relax.

'Family and friends have seen a difference in me, I am starting to laugh and joke again. The quality of my life has improved. I have started my keep-fit lessons again and I am now walking my dog. Generally, I am doing much more for myself and relying less on others. I still have pain but, with discipline and self-control, I rule my body and mind.

'I will not let the pain take over. Today, I take fewer pain-killers and hope to decrease them even more.

'At home, I am trying to forget the negative life I lived for three years. I am now positive again, in complete control. You can be in pain and enjoy life. With hard work and dedication, pain can be controlled without losing any of the quality of life.'

Barbara changed her life by developing a positive attitude and putting her pain in perspective. The patients in the trial on the exercise bikes had aches and pains the next day because they were unfit. Many chronic pain sufferers do not go dancing or bowling because they believe that the pain they may suffer next day indicates they have done themselves damage.

They will hurt, but only because they have not done it for so long. It is important to learn the difference between damage pain and post-exercise pain. If someone last danced 15 years ago, then they cannot possibly know if they cannot dance today. It may be difficult and something of an ordeal, but what they are really saying is that they *won't* dance. They have made a value judgement which is backed by fear, not fact. Their decision is that they simply will not be able to do it again.

What they should do is *un*-decide and tell themselves: 'I'd like to dance again. It's not going to be easy, but I'll try to see if I can work up to it.'

What we have here is another of pain's illusions. Pain encourages you to play safe so that it, not you, remains in control. The truth is that *hurt does not mean harm.* Chronic pain sufferers have a potential far greater than they imagine.

Almost every patient attending the Pain Management Programme doubles his or her activity level over four weeks. If they can continue to do that then, obviously, they have the potential to go on to greater things.

Having the right attitude to pain brings us back to locus of control – regaining control over yourself and the pain in your body. If you give up at the first twinge, then pain is running you.

People enrolling on pain programmes have an external locus of control, by which we mean that they expect other people to do things for them to help their pain. As soon as they are in pain, they stop doing things and allow pain to come through and dominate their lives. Learning to change your attitude means getting on with things and depressing the amount of pain which comes through for the length of a given activity. It means closing your pain gates and telling yourself that nothing will stop you getting on with this particular exercise.

The learning process is rather like wiggling your ears. We all obviously have innate abilities, like raising a leg or moving our toes. Others, such as being able to twitch your ears, are more hidden. Everyone has a muscle behind their ear and a nerve running from it to the brain. So, in theory, everyone should be able to wiggle their ears. However, not everyone knows how to do it in practice. Perhaps an average of one person in ten can perform this trick but, if you ask him to teach the other nine, he does not know where to begin. He has no idea *how* he does it, only that he can. The others agree that it is possible in theory, but somehow they can't.

In a similar way, the same ten people could close their pain gates and block a great proportion of their pain. They understand how it is possible to do it – that they all possess the mechanism to make it happen – but perhaps only one of them is able to put it into practice. Like juggling three balls, there is a difference between admiring someone's ability and acquiring the knack yourself.

When a thousand pain specialists attended an international conference in Florence, they broke after one of the sessions and wandered into the square outside the conference hall. A crowd was gathered round a man walking barefoot over broken glass and holding his feet in a candle flame. The pain doctors gathered round fascinated and asked if he felt anything.

The performer claimed he felt no pain at all. Then, one of the Italian pain specialists gave him some money and he talked more frankly about how he earned his living. He admitted that the glass and candle flame were quite painful, but he was able to suppress the pain because of the money he stood to collect at the end of each performance. No one in the crowd, or indeed, any of the doctors, could have withstood so much pain, but the performer was able to modify it because of that secondary gain. Releasing endorphins is not particularly magical or mysterious, it is simply a knack gained with experience.

Fakirs who lie on beds of nails, or fire-walkers who stroll over hot coals all withstand a certain amount of pain to achieve a goal. Beds of nails, for example, are made to precise specifications in which the nails are grouped closely to reduce the pain. If there were only half a dozen nails on the board, not even the most experienced Fakir could tolerate the pain.

The trick lies in reducing the amount of pain they allow through and coping with it. Such performers know they are not going to physically harm themselves because they have done it many times before and, often, seen their fathers and grandfathers do the same.

What helps them reduce the pain to an acceptable level is the reward at the end – it may be money, kudos, mental satisfaction or some kind of mystical experience. They still hurt, but the payback enables them to allow only a certain amount of pain through, which they can adequately cope with.

When we consider our pain gates, it is important to remember that those who can't close them are the ones who allow their lives to revolve entirely around the fact that they are ill and in pain. Their frustration begins when they discover that it is possible to close their pain gates and have less pain. They try, but nothing happens because their subconscious – which is always logical about such things – prevents them. 'Just a minute,' their subconscious insists. 'Your pain is important to you. You seem to need your pain gates open to allow as much pain through as possible to tell you something is wrong.'

So, the subconscious, quite rightly, reasons this way: 'You are asking me to close the gates and cut down pain, but I can't really believe you mean what you say. As soon as I open the gates and allow the pain through, you stop what you are doing and take a tablet. This tells me that pain is the most important thing in your life. You give it your full attention whenever it demands it. If you really didn't want to know about pain, you wouldn't take any notice.'

The subconscious is never going to learn to close the gates because the sufferers confirm they are ill by stopping whatever they are doing every time pain messages pass through.

The only way to effectively convince your subconscious is not to make promises, but to *live* in such a way that it believes you mean business. This means not grinding to a halt and giving up every time you feel a twinge of pain. It means setting yourself a target for a particular activity and accomplishing it, whether the pain comes through or not.

If, for example, you have decided to pedal an exercise bike for ten minutes, or to take a ten minute walk, it does not matter that you feel pain after six or eight minutes, you still have to go the distance and complete the ten minutes. If you have been assured medically that this cannot harm or damage you, then there is no reason to give in to pain any more.

Admitting defeat is not the easy way out. The sooner you give up before reaching your target, the chances are that you will feel more pain, not less, because you are giving your subconscious approval to let pain through. You have not convinced it that you really mean what you say. Give up early and your subconscious will argue: 'I knew you were going to feel pain after six minutes, so next time I will open the gates after five minutes to warn you not to push yourself too far.'

Given the opportunity, your subconscious becomes one of those annoying people who think they know best and try to organize your life for you.

There are times when you have to be insistent, to put your foot down and prove that you are in charge. Otherwise, on the next occasion, your subconscious will decide to open the gates after four minutes to play safe, and so on. The more easily you give up, the more painful it becomes and any progress you had hoped to make slides backwards.

Having decided on your target, it becomes vitally important to stick to it. You may find that the activity is easier than you thought and you feel you can go on for 12 minutes. This is almost as bad as giving up early, because you are cheating your subconscious.

You have to prove that when you say something you mean it. If you made a deal for ten minutes and exceeded it, your subconscious becomes confused. It prepared itself to keep the gates closed for ten minutes because it knew that you were determined to stick to your decision. As soon as you increased the time, it believed that you were no longer in control and felt that it might as well open the gates at three minutes as twelve.

Setting targets means:

- Thinking through what you intend to do
- Taking complete control of yourself
- Having the right attitude
- Sticking to what you say

It does not mean vague, open-ended activity plans, such as: 'I think I'll do some gardening.' For all your subconscious knows, you could mean 16 hours. Naturally, it will go into a panic and turn up the pain after 30 minutes to stop you going too far.

Half an hour today, 40 minutes tomorrow, perhaps 45 minutes the following day is an arrangement your subconscious may find more attractive than an open-ended contract. Once you have made a deal with yourself, never give in early and never get carried away by euphoria and cheat.

Your subconscious is like a jobsworth, one of those irritating minor officials who stick to the rules. He is trying to do his job to the best of his ability because you have made it clear that pain is the most important thing in your life. Once you decide otherwise, and change direction, he has to know exactly where he stands at each stage of the way to do his job efficiently.

Your subconscious will take the cue from you: as long as it is convinced you mean what you say. Behaving as though pain is no longer significant diminishes its importance in your life. Your subconscious, like the good servant it is, will react accordingly by reducing the amount of pain allowed through the gates. Once it becomes convinced that pain is no longer central to your existence, it will stop opening the gates to warn you that you might hurt yourself. There is no point because, as far as your subconscious is concerned, you are no longer interested.

By setting reasonable, positive goals you can influence your subconscious and increase the amount of activity you wish to do.

Ellen, 54, was in so much pain that she could not stand the touch of clothes on her back. Eventually, she joined a Pain Management Programme:

> 'Instead of feeling alone, frightened and suicidal, I was shown various methods of self-help and was amazed at the difference they made to my life. I still have chronic pain every single day but, rather than dwell on all the things I once enjoyed doing, I find other ways around it. For instance, I gave up typing because of the pain in my hands from arthritis. By setting myself targets, I bought myself an electric typewriter and was thrilled when people in the village asked me to type for them. I have now enrolled for a course in word processing so that I can extend my interests.'

Terry, a bus driver who suffers from chronic back pain:

> 'For years, I avoided using my left hand and arm because I thought I would automatically give myself more pain. This has been proved incorrect. My plans now are to continue with exercises, as I didn't realise how unfit I was until I started doing them. I have just begun to go swimming again – a marvellous exercise and one which I had simply got out of the habit of doing.'

Kay suffered chest pains following a pulmonary embolism:

> 'I felt desperate. Desperate at the way in which fear of pain was taking my life over. I had stopped exercising a long time ago in case I made the pain worse. I avoided making social engagements for fear of not being well enough to go. In the end, friends became fed-up with me cancelling dates.
>
> 'Understanding the psychology of pain has really helped me. I realise how protective of my body I had become and I am thankful I am now through the barrier. I am less fearful and analytical of my pain because I know I have the tools to cope with it.'

Pain sufferers who cope by setting themselves targets know that they may have good and bad days. Anticipating the troughs when pain can make activity more difficult than usual is an important part of the psychology. It is advisable to prepare yourself by scaling down activity to ride through the trough. If bad pain days mean that you only achieve, say, half your targets, then it is perfectly reasonable to lower them and work up again when you are heading for a peak.

In the 1960s, doctors treated pain with the theory that many conditions could be improved by surgery. If your back hurt, the idea was to 'nail' it together again. When that failed to work, the answer was to 'nail' it better, harder, bigger. This continued until a realization evolved that the approach was of little permanent help. In America, doctors were also worried because so many patients were taking legal action against them because they were too easily resorting to surgery which simply did not work.

Medical opinion came to the conclusion that there were other reasons why pain patients continued to suffer – pain was multi-factorial.

Pain came to be viewed as behaviour in the way that accent is a kind of behaviour. Someone may speak with a regional accent because people around them spoke the same way when they were children and they felt that it was the best way to behave. Similarly, if a child from, say, London emigrated to Canada, he would subtly adopt a Canadian accent as a way of relating to other children.

He would not modify his accent on account of his parents, because he would feel secure in their love and affection, but because he felt unsure of other children. It would be easier to change and fit in with them.

Ever since Pavlov trained dogs to salivate by associating the sound of a bell with food, doctors have been aware that behaviour can be changed. The same subconscious conditioned response that made Pavlov's dogs drool can produce pain in people, under certain circumstances.

In the 1960s, American pain researchers concluded that if you had acute pain and were off work, receiving sickness benefit and behaving like an invalid, your family took notice of you. You acquired a pain behaviour which, in time, might go on to become chronic pain.

A patient from the Isle of Man attending the Pain Management Programme provided a vivid demonstration of conditioning. Although his original illness had disappeared, he found that a day's work generated a tremendous amount of pain. By the time he got home in the evening and sat in his recliner chair, the pain was unbearable. On the Pain Management Programme, the exercise and physical activity were much greater than at work, yet he hardly felt any pain when he sat down to rest. The culprit turned out to be the recliner chair, which conditioned his behaviour because it had so many pain associations. When he returned to the Isle of Man, he threw the chair out and never experienced pain on such an intense level again.

Based on the conviction that pain was learned, early programmes took the approach of making patients un-learn their behaviour, which in many ways was not very different to unsophisticated brainwashing. The system, now abandoned in its pure form, has merits when used in other areas. Children in hospital, for example, may come from homes where they have learned that the only way to get attention is to be naughty. Hospital staff take a behavioural approach by ignoring them when they are naughty and giving them the attention they crave when they are good.

In a similar way a baby can quickly learn that, when it cries its mother will pick it up. If it cried louder, she will pick it up more quickly. This 'screech behaviour', as it is known, can be overcome by picking up the baby when it is peaceful. The baby learns that it will be picked up when it is quiet and left when it screams.

Early pain programmes revolved almost entirely around the principle that patients would be ignored when they complained of pain. They were told that if they did things positively, they would get attention. If they writhed on the floor in agony, staff would step over them. What's more, they would teach the patient's family to do the same.

The psychology was tough and ultimately in the patient's interest, but constituted only a small part of a complete approach to pain relief. Its shortcoming was that patients were all being tagged with the same behavioural label when, in fact, their conditions were very diverse.

The Japanese developed a similar behavioural system called 'The School of Bravery' in which patients with conditions such as rheumatoid arthritis were made to walk and run. When they were asked how they felt, they probably replied: 'It hurts like hell. But I'm being very brave.' Conditioning people to change their behaviour is not the whole answer. Motivation has to come from within by combining positive attitude with exercise, relaxation and understanding the psychology of pain.

The modern approach to pain management began when patients on behavioural courses began to talk to psychologists and ask if there weren't other ways of achieving the same ends. One of the first methods of broadening programmes was to introduce relaxation, which is a cognitive approach, as opposed to conditioning. Cognition means discovering about ourselves and enabled a patient to realize that, when his back hurt, he could make himself more relaxed and therefore feel less pain. 'Right attitude' began to play a central role in learning how to manage pain.

The Pain Management Programme at Walton Hospital developed from an awareness that patients were not responding to other treatments. It operated in the belief that patients needed to become fit, to relax and to learn more about themselves. As the programme developed, we accepted the importance of other therapies, some of which were not generally recognized, and the therapeutic value of working in groups.

Patients also needed reassuring that the staff genuinely believed they were in pain – that they were not malingering or complaining for no reason. In turn, patients had to understand that their pain was not simply a physical experience, there were emotional and psychological ramifications that could make it worse. Until they understood that, their condition could not improve. They had to recognize, too, that they could not rely on drugs and, if they continued to take large quantities, they would feel worse. Removing this psychological crutch was an important step towards learning right attitude. Combining these lessons and applying them diligently continues to bring about remarkable changes in outlook.

Betty, who attended the programme, had suffered from back pain since the birth of her daughter in 1974:

'During the birth, I was given an epidural injection which went wrong. Two pieces of catheter broke off in my back, causing severe back pain and a loss of feeling in my leg. Two weeks later, I had an operation in which the surgeon managed to remove one of the pieces.

'Over the following nine months, I had problems with the operation scar because stitches, inserted deep in my back, were being rejected and causing an infection. I had to have surgery again to remove all the stitches and clean the wound. These two operations on my spine caused a weakness, in addition to the back pain and loss of feeling in my leg.

'In the early 1980s, I took a job in a warehouse assembling orders of drugs for chemists' shops, but had to leave because my back pain was so severe.

'Around 1985, an orthopaedic surgeon made some attempts to inject cortisone into my spine, but the treatment did not work. He advised my GP to send me to the Pain Relief Clinic. Various methods of controlling the pain by treating nerve ends and removing scar tissue were tried, but I was finally told that the pain could not be cured.

'At the time I joined the Pain Management Programme I was taking Coproxamol, naprosyn and paracetamol when I was in severe pain. My activity was very low. I stayed in bed late in the mornings.

'I did not go out to the shops and did not often visit my friends. At the start of the course I was depressed, fed-up, angry, irritable and had lost all my confidence.

'One of the targets I achieved was to go out to the shops on my own. I also plan to go out more often socially and visit my family and friends.

'More than anything, I have changed emotionally and now have a different, positive outlook on life. As a result, I feel happier and not as irritable and angry. My husband and children have noticed a big difference in my attitude. I feel more complete again.'

REMBEMBER

Make regular, realistic targets in all departments of your life. Setting targets means.

- Thinking through what you intend to do.
- Taking complete control of yourself.
- Having the right attitude.
- Sticking to what you say.

4

The importance of a healthy body – exercise and diet

Exercise is one of the most powerful weapons in the fight against pain. Swimming, walking, gentle aerobics and similar activities all release endorphins, which not only help you overcome pain, but make exercise fun. They bring about a feeling of well-being that many pain sufferers forget they once possessed. Without exercise, even the fittest of us become depressed. A doctor attached to the Pain Clinic was an outstanding schoolboy cricketer for India. When he enrolled at medical school he decided that there was no time for both study and cricket, and gave up his favourite sport.

Within three months he became increasingly depressed without understanding the reason and, at one time, even contemplated suicide. He was advised that it was because he had given up the exercise which had become an integral part of his life.

He worked out a programme of jogging to the hospital five mornings a week, not because he was unfit, but to keep himself from becoming depressed. By creating a niche in his life for exercise, he regained his happiness.

Professional sportsmen and women who exercise regularly often become low in spirits if they break a leg and have to stay on the injury list. Star athletes who strain a tendon often feel they will never attain peak form again because they feel depressed at being out of training. They find it hard to believe in themselves when they are laid up. Everyone has to believe in themselves and being unfit through pain takes this away from us.

When you are in pain it is difficult not to be over-protective of yourself. This is true of acute pain – if you break your leg or have angina, you wouldn't try to run upstairs.

With chronic pain it is manifestly not the case. In recent years medicine has tended to move away from a negative outlook on pain and recovery and become much more positive. A generation ago, someone recovering from a heart attack would be in hospital for up to a month. Staff would very gingerly get them out of bed after three or four days and, frankly, worry about them dropping dead.

Twenty years before, the approach was even more cautious. A heart patient would be hospitalised for six weeks and confined to bed for half that period, with strict orders not to move. They were warned that their heart was so bad that when they were finally allowed out of bed, they would be breathless. We realize now, of course, that anyone would be breathless after three weeks in bed, because they would be unfit.

Today heart attack patients are admitted to hospital and, providing there are no complications, find themselves in a chair the same day. Ten days in hospital is now not uncommon for a heart attack victim. In times past they would not have been properly mobilised by then.

A similarly progressive view is being taken with orthopaedic problems. A decade ago, a footballer who had to have a knee operation would have been in plaster for six weeks, followed by another six weeks physiotherapy to break down the adhesions from the plaster. One famous footballer recently had a knee operation and was playing at Wembley four weeks later.

When someone has a cartilage removed, activity is going to be painful, but doctors take the view that it will certainly do no harm to exercise within a week. Some greenstick fractures in children are now not even put in plaster. If the child can use his arm, and no dislocating force is going to be applied to it, then it is more beneficial to be able to move it around.

Exercise is vital because it helps to overcome pain and fight the depression immobility brings.

As the treatment of acute pain has become more aggressive with regard to getting patients quickly back on their feet, the approach to chronic pain needs to move even further in that direction. One reason is that the chronic pain sufferer may have been encouraged by his GP and family not to exercise. Those around them quickly become over-solicitous ('Don't do the garden, dear – you might hurt yourself' ... 'Leave the dishes, I'll do them for you' ...) turning them into an invalid and making them unfit.

A psychologist working at a university in Scotland was

referred to the Pain Clinic suffering from tension and depression. The problem had begun with sciatica, caused by disc disease in his back. While it was possible to operate on him, his doctor had decided it might be unwise because he had mild haemophilia and ran a risk of bleeding. When he complained that the pain was terrible, he was advised not to be as active, because it was obviously not good for him.

This was bad news for the psychologist because he and his wife ran a rural smallholding with five acres of vegetables to till, chickens that needed feeding and a cow which had to be milked twice a day. Afraid of ignoring the doctor's advice, he stopped doing everything and became very depressed. His wife had twice the amount of work to do and soon there was friction between them, which made him tense and even more depressed.

As a psychologist, he understood his condition – he was tense because his lifestyle had been changed and from being active, he was now afraid to do anything. When he was examined there was no manifestation of any disc disease he might once have had. It appeared that the surgeon did not want to operate because of his haemophilia and advised him to give up physical work as a safety precaution to justify his position.

I told the patient that there was no evidence that any exercise would harm him in any way and asked him what he really wanted.

'All I want,' he replied, 'is an assurance that I can safely go back and work on my smallholding.'

I took a sheet of headed notepaper and wrote the words: 'You can go back and work on your smallholding,' and handed it to him.

'This is exactly what I needed,' he said. 'Permission for my subconscious to make it happen.'

Six months later, he wrote to say that he was happy again,

his relationship with his wife was back to normal and he had found renewed energy for his work at the university. On his tour of doctors, all he ever wanted was permission to exercise and, because he was denied it, his life had fallen apart.

The classic slogan here relating to muscle is 'Use It Or Lose It'. If you do not exercise there is the strongest likelihood that you will embark on a dreary cycle of depression and pain. Even the healthiest person will have muscle weakness and back pain if they spend most of their time in bed or in a chair.

Once you believe that you can exercise safely without harm, the problem is how do you know how far to go?

Firstly, there is no question of going out and running a personal marathon. Even the fittest athletes suffer from stretching themselves too far. The first step is to set a goal you want to achieve and build up towards it in attainable stages.

If, for example, you would like to take up swimming again, make your first step going to the baths to float on your back and splash around. Have a little fun in the water before getting out. As much as you desperately want to swim 16 lengths, it is important that you do not even try. On your second visit, you could perhaps aim to swim a width and the next time, two widths. If you find that easy or encouraging, then try a couple of lengths on the following occasion. If that proves too much, revert to widths again until you feel ready for greater things.

The idea is to create your exercise programme in tiny units that you are sure of achieving. Always aim for the simplest goals to increase your fitness, confidence and well-being. By doing so your progress will always be positive and moving steadily forward.

You may find that pain has prevented you from driving your car and the target you have chosen is to drive to visit some friends. For the first stage, don't even pick up your car keys. Simply walk to the car and sit behind the wheel for a while. It may be a modest goal, but it is the first step towards driving again.

The second time you get in the car, switch on the engine but don't attempt to drive anywhere. On the next occasion, when you are used to the idea of being in charge of a vehicle again, you can drive ten yards down the block. Walk home and ask someone else to move the car back for you. To begin with, it is important only to go forwards.

Break your target into small steps which are easy to accomplish and log them on a chart so that you can see yourself progressing closer to your goal of driving to London and back. It may take a year, but you are not seeking great leaps of improvement. Far better to stick to a time scale which assures you of success.

Each step you take, you are making yourself active and taking gentle exercise. If you do not exercise you face two debilitating problems – muscle weakness and shortening of the ligaments.

When muscles become weak with under-use, even the slightest form of activity can make you tired. When ligaments shorten and you take up exercise to stretch them, they become inflamed. Both of these conditions tend to cause pain, if not at the time, then almost certainly next day.

Many pain sufferers are not incapable of simple exercise such as mowing the lawn. If they really had to do it, they probably could. What prevents them is retribution fear; the knowledge that they will wake up next morning feeling miserable because they are in pain.

What this indicates is simply aching muscles and ligaments, not a worsening of the original pain. It is something professional athletes and footballers feel after every event. The time to take notice is when you experience a new pain, or worsening of your pain as you are exercising.

If, for example, someone takes a walk and feels a new pain

shooting down his leg, then he is probably right to stop and check with his GP. He might have intermittent claudication (cramping pain caused by poor circulation), vascular problems or even something wrong with a disc.

The point is that this is acute pain which is occurring at the time and preventing him from doing his particular activity. Pain which is felt the next day simply means that you are unfit; it is harmless and can be overcome.

You may accept this and put the pain in perspective, but the thought remains: is it worth going through it? The answer depends upon how much you wish to improve the quality of your life.

When women pain sufferers complain that they get pain when they go out and enjoy themselves, we often discover that it is equally painful to stay at home and do the housework. If that is the case, and you feel you can only tackle one activity, then go out and enjoy yourself and worry about the housework later. There is little point in only doing housework and not enjoying it because you are not going to improve. Now and again, it is more important to go out and have fun to improve the quality of your life and your sense of achievement and well-being.

This is not an easy decision to make. Some women frankly prefer to stay at home and do the housework because they consider it more important. What they are choosing to do is to have their pain and be miserable, rather than have it and, for a few hours, be happy. If pain dominates your life, consider changing your routine and adopting a new approach. If you go out socially, you can still attempt the housework next day.

The pain will be the same but, as you work, you will feel better within yourself. You have refused to allow pain to gain the upper hand and taken a positive step towards overcoming it.

The benefit of exercise is not only physical, enabling you to become fitter and release endorphins, it also improves your self-image. Suddenly, from not being able to drive the car, or swim, or dance, it means that you are doing the things you have missed. Even participating in them a little is better than not achieving anything at all.

Those who lack the courage to try are held back by fear and worry. They allow pain to win its battle against them and will continue to feel inadequate, angry and depressed. Activity releases endorphins which not only reduce pain, but make you feel good and give you the confidence to do more.

Having the right attitude actually helps produce endorphins, too. Whether your motive is pride, determination or a cussed refusal to be a victim of pain for the rest of your life, you are taking positive steps to taking control of your pain.

Marathon runners face the same problem constantly when, towards the end of a race, they encounter 'the wall' – the point when they are in so much pain that they are desperate to drop out and give up. They know, as professionals, that they can either quit or produce endorphins to take them through the barrier and enable them to finish. At that moment, their decision hinges on attitude.

Despite training hard and being exceptionally fit, every marathon runner reaches this crisis in a race. What pushes them on is self-commitment. A Liverpool footballer took part in the city's annual marathon and was in such pain that he was on the point of signalling the ambulance. Ahead of him, he saw a man in his sixties, still going on and clearly determined to finish. The player thought: 'If he can do it at his age, so can I,' and summoned the reserves he needed to pass the finishing line.

Once you reach that point, it is as though your subconscious, which has been urging you to play safe and give up, suddenly realises that you mean business and decides to offer all the help it can. In daily life, your subconscious will always persuade you to capitulate to pain because it knows you are afraid of harming yourself. Once you stamp your authority upon it and prove your determination, it will produce the endorphins to carry you through. Afterwards, you will feel better – for the same reason that marathon runners are elated when they finish a race. Endorphins not only help you to break through the wall of pain, but make you feel good in the process.

The 400 metres is acknowledged to be one of the most demanding races in athletics. For the first 300 metres, the runner's training carries him through. At 310 metres he has a burning in his chest not unlike a major heart attack. At this stage, he knows that he still has some distance to go. The question he has to ask himself is whether he can put up with the pain for another ten seconds. His subconscious tells him that, if he stops, it will go away. Experience tells him that if he listens, his next race will be even more difficult. As soon as he decides to complete the final 90 metres, the pain becomes less important.

Like athletes, pain sufferers have to believe in themselves. Working alone is not easy, which is precisely why all sportsmen have a coach to motivate them and give them the incentive to break through the pain. Exercising with others is not only more fun, but more effective.

You do not have to join a keep-fit group for disabled people if you are in pain. Any kind of swimming, walking or pop-mobility group will do, as long as you explain your condition and make it clear to the instructor that you will only be able to work at a low initial rate. The danger of some go-for-the-burn style exercise groups is that they encourage participants to work flat-out. If you try to compete, there is a real danger of hurting yourself, which is not the right approach when you are in chronic pain.

Build up gradually and never exercise until you hurt if you

suffer chronic pain or else you will almost certainly damage muscles. When you exercise with others, select your group carefully so that you can obtain maximum benefit. T'ai Chi and yoga are excellent in this respect. Many civic sports centres now provide exercise for the elderly, passive exercise to music or movement in water (aquarobics) at local swimming baths.

In groups of this kind you will not feel pressure to keep up or worry that you are being left behind. It is always important to avoid placing yourself in a negative situation. Other members, who are healthy and not suffering pain, must appreciate that you may be a little slower. Set out your own ground rules before you take part. Explain that you will only be swimming half a length and after two weeks you hope to be swimming a length. There is no way in which you will be able to swim 40 lengths with the rest of them.

When they see that you have your own programme and targets, people in the group with the right attitude will give all the support they can. The value of joining is that people who care pick you up when you are down. After coping with pain on your own, it is a joy to answer the phone and hear someone say: 'We missed you last week, couldn't you make it?'

All kinds of people, from weight watchers to alcoholics, know that they receive more support and make more personal progress with understanding people around them. Few people who read this book will be able to overcome pain alone without any kind of outside assistance. The social aspect of conquering pain is extremely important. If, for example, you are unable to join a relaxation group, then perhaps going to church and relaxing there would be of some benefit.

Making the effort to get up and go out, to become more active socially, is a target which works in harmony with exercise and relaxation. One of the most common problems in the elderly, for example, is loneliness. Old ladies with back pain who join the Pain Management Programme tend to require little treatment.

By the end of the third or fourth week many are laughing as they exercise because there is finally some point in doing it. At home, there seemed to be little incentive.

The point to consider about working on muscles and ligaments is that the type of exercise you choose doesn't matter as long as it has value for you. If you are frightened of water, then there is little value in swimming. Some people say they enjoy ten-pin bowling and, while it may not exactly score high on everyone's recommendation list, if it is fun for the sufferers and keeps them active, then it will produce positive results in their fight against pain. Whatever form of exercise you choose, the release of endorphins will be a tangible morale-booster.

Gentle exercise will cut down the pain you are suffering. It is not enough for muscles and ligaments that you do the housework or walk to the shops. Exercise programmes strengthen muscles which are normally under-used and help to stabilise the spine.

When you exercise it is important to remember to follow through the full extent of any movement because, quite often, it is the last part of the action which carries the benefit. If you are asked to straighten your arm, or stretch your neck, really try to follow the instructions as fully as you are able.

Just as many myths surround pain, there are quite a few fallacies concerning exercise. If you suffer from arthritis or rheumatism, your joints do not wear out with over-use! In fact, it is much better to use them than to sit in a chair all day as this causes stiffness.

If you find that exercise is causing you pain in your joints, there is a possibility that you are doing too much. Little and often is better than prolonged exercise periods. The Arthritis and Rheumatism Council advise doing housework and gardening in short spells interrupted by short rests. It is equally important not to sit in one place for too long – from time to time get up and stretch your joints.

Exercise is also of enormous benefit to patients suffering from myofascial pain which is caused by muscles developing tender fibrous nodules called trigger points. Pressure on these points can give rise to a characteristic aching pain. While the problem may be treated by acupuncture, local anaesthetic injections, acupressure and 'spray and stretch' therapy, exercise is the key to sustained relief.

Specific exercises which relieve myofascial pain provide a good general warm-up to a sustained exercise programme. Basic rules for avoiding myofascial pain are also sound advice to all pain sufferers:

Never bend and lift, or pull something with the back twisted.

Always lift with the knees bent, holding your back in an erect forward-facing position.

Never get up from a chair, or sit down, while leaning forward in a stooped position with the trunk rotated.

STRETCHING EXERCISES FOR MYOFASCIAL PAIN

These are easy stretching exercises, working from the neck down to your bottom. They are not comprehensive, but may help you choose appropriate exercises and help other chronic pain sufferers loosen up before joining an exercise programme.

General neck and back stretching:

Sit with your legs straight out, if you can. Bend your body forward, as if to touch your toes. (You could also place both hands behind your head, which also stretches your back.) If you are very stiff, breathe deeply and let your tummy push you slightly backwards. Then, when you breathe out, let the motion carry your body further forwards, a little with each breath.

Neck stretching:

Bend your neck forward to touch your chin to your chest. You can combine this with deep breathing, allowing your chin to drop forward a little with each breath. Move your left ear towards your shoulder, with your face facing forward, then repeat on the opposite side. Touch your chin to your left shoulder and do the same on the opposite side. Then move your occiput – the back of your head – towards your left shoulder and repeat for the opposite side. You will find that these exercises will draw the different muscles of your neck to a stretch.

Shoulder and chest muscle stretch:

Stand in a doorway with your arms outstretched on both door posts. Lean slightly forward on your toes and take your weight on your arms, stretching up to your chest (pectoral muscles). If you place your arms upwards, you will stretch the lower muscle fibres; placing your arms downwards stretches the upper muscle fibres.

To stretch your shoulder muscles, you can put your arm across the opposite shoulder, as if to scratch your back. Use your other arm to push your elbow as far as you can towards the opposite shoulder. Repeat for the opposite arm.

Now try placing the arm behind your chest and use the opposite arm to pull it across as far as possible.

To stretch the muscles at the back of your chest, hug yourself tightly and take a deep breath.

Side stretch:

Stand with your legs slightly apart, look straight ahead and bend slightly to your left. Try to bring your left hand as far down your thigh as possible. To add further stretch at the same time, you can place your right arm over your head, towards the opposite side. Repeat the stretch towards your right side.

Exercising with others is preferable to exercising alone but, if you are unable to join a group, any exercise is better than none. The four-week exercise programme, devised by physiotherapists for Walton Hospital's Pain Management Programme, provides a good framework. The aim is to work all your muscles, building up the number of repetitions of each movement as the course progresses.

Remember, there is no hurry. You should avoid speed or sudden jerky movements. Exercise is fun and the objective is to feel better afterwards. The number in brackets after each movement is a guide to how many times it may be repeated the first time you exercise:

Standing and Sitting Exercises

Touch toes: If you find you can't reach your toes, extend as far as you comfortably can (*three times*).

Alternate knee bend: In a standing position, lift your knee as high as you can in the direction of your chest (*five times*).

Lateral bending: Stand and bend your upper body sideways until it is at right angles to your legs (*five times*).

Arm circle: Stand and make the biggest circle possible with your arm, then repeat with the other (*five times*).

Step ups: Step on and off the first step of your stairs. If you happen to live in a bungalow, try the back-door step or a bench instead! (*five times*).

Wall slide: Stand with your back against a smooth wall. Slide down into a squatting position and repeat (*five times*).

Push ups against the wall: Stand facing a wall, arms' length away from it.

Place your hands against the wall at chest height. Lean forward and slowly push yourself away until your arms are straight (*five times*).

Forward stretch: Stand and place one foot on a chair or stool. Lean forward to stretch your leg and back muscles (*five times*).

Stand/sit: Sit on a chair, stand and sit down again (*five times*).

Chair push ups: Sit in a chair and push on the arms to raise your bottom from the seat (*five times*).

Lying Face Up

Ankles up and down: Raise your leg a few inches and move your foot forward and backward (*five times*).

Ankle circling: Raise your leg a few inches and rotate your foot (*five times*).

Alternate straight raises: Raise your leg as high as you can, keeping it straight. Repeat with the other leg (*three times*).

Lying Knees Bent, Feet on the Mat

Flatten back: When we lie down we tend to have an arch in our lower back. Move your pelvis until the whole of your back makes contact with the floor, and repeat (*five times*).

Alternate hand to knee: This is somewhat self-explanatory – touch your left knee with your right hand and then repeat in the opposite direction, left hand to right knee (*five times*).

Alternate arm stretch: Lie with your arms at your sides and raise each arm in turn, stretching as high as you can (*Five times*).

Lying on Right Side, Then Left Side

Leg Raise: Raise your leg vertically as high as you can manage (*three times*).

Lying Face Down

Alternate leg raise: Try to lift one leg, then the other (*three times*).
Push ups: Place your palms on the floor, on either side of your chest, and push yourself up until your arms are straight. Start by bending from the knees (*three times*).

Another recommended exercise programme is the Royal Canadian Air Force book *Physical Fitness.*

Being unfit and being tense go hand in hand. Most patients arrive at the Pain Clinic both out of condition and suffering from obvious muscle tension. This is quite understandable because pain changes their posture, making their muscles work harder to hold the shape which their pain has dictated. Some people arrive bent over, others twisted into positions which they believe gives them less discomfort. When they try to sit straight it hurts because their ligaments have become shortened. To stay in the position shaped by their pain means using certain groups of muscles much harder than others. The result is that some muscles are taut and in constant tension, while others are weak and under-used. Most are unaware of this muscle spasm.

In addition, they are suffering from the anxiety and stress of their new life as an invalid. They worry about their future, their income, relationships with their family, as well as how pain is affecting them physically and mentally. Such problems are enough to make anyone tense but for chronic pain sufferers it has become a way of life and many never even realise that their muscles are not relaxed.

Quite often, they say that pain prevents them from leading a normal life because they feel so tired all the time. On close examination, it is often the case that they are fatigued because their muscles are constantly working at full stretch to no useful end. Many people think that muscle tension cannot be anything serious. You raise your arm horizontally, tensing the muscles, and it does not particularly hurt. Try to hold it in that position for five minutes, however, and it becomes agony.

Muscles quickly go into spasm when they are subjected to extreme tension. In Canada, I was called out one Sunday morning to a 6 foot 6 inch lumberjack who was writhing on the floor in pain with a pulled back muscle. He was big and fit and strong and looked as though he consumed 6000 calories a day (6000 calories for breakfast would not have surprised me), yet he was crying like a baby.

He had torn a muscle in his back and the muscles around it had gone into spasm. He was in so much pain that he had to be given an intravenous sedative to give his muscles time to relax. When he came round, the pain was considerably reduced. Even for a man so obviously fit, muscle spasm can hurt terribly.

An anaesthetic called Scoline is used in operating theatres for certain surgical procedures. It makes all the muscles go into spasm for a few seconds until they burn up energy, exhaust themselves and then totally relax.

It is not unusual for patients who have this anaesthetic, especially those with good muscles, to present themselves at a hospital casualty department 24 or 48 hours later with all the signs of a coronary thrombosis. They complain of chest pains, turn very pale and, if the hospital is unaware of their operation, the staff could quite easily think the patient has had a heart attack. The condition wears off in a few days but, at the time, is very real and severe pain caused by contraction of the muscles.

Relaxation in the sense of having conscious control over your muscles is an important part of exercise. Engaging in physical activity and simply allowing your muscles to slacken and rest is not enough. It has the same effect as sitting in front of the TV after a day's work. You think you are relaxed, but your muscles can be tense while your subconscious drifts from one negative thought to another. What has really happened is that your conscious has taken a vacation.

Managing pain is being in control, whether doing exercise or relaxing. If you are doing nothing, you are giving pain an opportunity to regain control. Real relaxation involves your conscious telling the rest of your body exactly how it wants it to be. Learning to relax means closing the door on pain, even when you are at rest. This is one example of having an internal locus of control.

Inactivity caused by chronic pain may also lead to obesity and other complications, especially if you are prone to arthritis. The Arthritis and Rheumatism Council for Research advises dieting to reduce strain on joints and increase mobility:

'People who are overweight are more likely to develop

osteo-arthritis,' they state. 'When you are walking, your hips and knee joints carry at least four times your body weight, so it is not surprising that osteo-arthritis in the legs causes more problems for people who are too heavy. However, the arthritis is not caused simply because these joints cannot bear the load. People who are overweight are also more likely to develop osteo-arthritis in their fingers and hands.

'Losing weight will not only reduce the load on painful joints, it will also improve your ability to get about and exercise more. This helps you feel less sluggish and enables you to burn off more calories. Losing weight is never easy, but shedding even a few pounds will help. You will find general health improves, as well as your arthritis.'

Other weight-related problems include high blood pressure, diabetes, gall-bladder disease, breathing problems and varicose veins.

Choosing to eat a healthy diet will not only help you to control your weight, but also may help to prevent a number of other health problems which are common in the Western world, including heart disease and stroke, dental caries (tooth decay), bowel disorders and certain cancers.

What is a healthy diet?

- Eating a variety of foods.
- One that maintains a healthy weight.
- Eating less fats and watching the type of fat.
- Eating plenty of starchy foods, especially those high in fibre.
- Eating plenty of fruit, vegetables and salads.

- Eating less sugar.
- Alcohol should be taken only in moderation.

It is recommended that a variety of foods should be taken because this reduces the risk of any nutritional deficiencies. Whilst you can live on a few foods and have a very healthy diet, unless you have some knowledge of nutrition, it may be by luck rather than by design. Many of the so-called 'cure-all' diets, often advocated in magazines, can lead to nutrition problems.

How do I know if I am overweight?

Most people know whether they are overweight or putting on weight, but it is wise to have an occasional weight check to ensure that the pounds are not gradually creeping on. It is always easier to lose a little weight than to have to mount a long-term campaign.

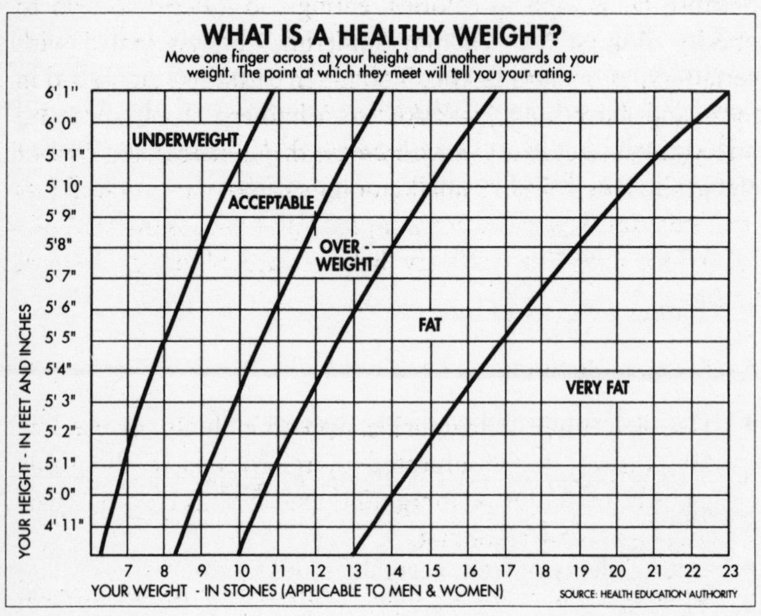

If you are overweight – how can you slim?

- By reducing your fat and sugar intake.
- Avoiding snacking between meals.
- Avoiding or reducing your alcohol intake.
- Eating plenty of high-fibre foods, including fruit and vegetables.

If you are underweight – does it matter?
If the chart (on page 92) indicates that you are underweight, it may be wise to discuss this with your doctor. It may be that you have no appetite and/or you may be eating foods which give you insufficient energy. If there is a problem, your doctor may refer you to a dietician for advice.

Eating less fat and watching types of fat:
Because fat is high in calories, eating too much will lead to obesity. A high fat diet may sometimes be associated with certain types of cancers, too. Too much saturated fat, found in meat and dairy foods, is linked to a higher risk of heart and artery disease because it may increase the cholesterol (a type of fat) in the blood. Using small amounts of polyunsaturated fats (fish oils, sunflower oil, corn oil, etc.) and monosaturated fats (olive oil, rapeseed oil) may help reduce blood cholesterol levels.

How do I do this?

- Use less butter or margarine. Spread it thinly, or use low fat spread. Polyunsaturated margarines have the same calories as butter or margarine and should be used sparingly if you are slimming.
- Change to fat-reduced milk (skimmed or semi-skimmed

milk). Remember, if the family are using this, too, children under the age of five should not be given fat-reduced milk.

- Try to eat less full fat cheese and use half fat cheese or cottage cheese instead. Avoid eating cheese between meals.
- Use low fat yoghurt or skimmed milk 'Fromage Frais' instead of cream.
- Cut down on high fat snacks – crisps, chocolate, cakes, biscuits, pastries.
- Avoid fried foods – grill, microwave, boil, poach, bake or steam instead.
- Eat more fish. All fish is good for you, especially the oily varieties, such as mackerel and herring.
- Use more chicken or turkey, but avoid the skin because most of the fat is there.
- Buy lean cuts of meat and trim off any visible fat. Eat fewer burgers and sausages, or try to buy 'lower fat' varieties. Eat smaller portions of meat and add more vegetables, including beans, peas or barley, to stews.
- Skim off the fat from mince, stews and soups by removing it with absorbent kitchen paper, or allow it to cool and remove the fat when cold (remember to thoroughly re-heat again).
- Limit eggs to three or four a week.
- Avoid chips and roast potatoes – eat boiled or baked potatoes instead, preferably in their skins.
- Use lemon juice or vinegar on salads instead of salad cream and mayonnaise.

- Avoid ice-cream (dairy and non-dairy fat varieties). There are some very low fat ice-creams available, which may be suitable in small quantities if you are slimming – read their labels.

If you are not overweight:
You are still advised to limit your fat intake. For baking, you could use either margarines high in polyunsaturates or olive oil fat spreads. For sauces and salad dressings use an oil high in polyunsaturates (sunflower, safflower, corn oil) or monosaturates (olive or rapeseed oil). Always use a suitable oil for frying and do not re-use it more than twice. It is advisable to cut down on chips and, when you do have them, cut them thickly. If you buy frozen chips, choose those cooked in sunflower or similar oil. Similarly with crisps, cut down the amount you eat and buy only those cooked in sunflower-type oils.

Starchy Foods

These provide the energy for your diet. Unless you are overweight and advised to limit (not avoid) these foods, they should be taken in good amounts. Starchy foods high in fibre will help to regulate your bowels and some may help reduce your blood cholesterol. If you are prone to constipation – a frequent problem if you take pain killers containing codeine or similar preparations – a high fibre diet may be particularly beneficial, as well as a high fluid intake.

Which starchy foods should I choose?

- Eat plenty of bread, especially wholemeal or bran enriched.
- Eat more boiled or baked potatoes, preferably in their skins.

- Include breakfast cereals, especially whole-grain varieties such as porridge, Weetabix, Shredded wheat, muesli, bran-flakes and oat cereals.
- Eat more rice, especially brown rice.
- Try more pasta, especially the brown varieties.
- If you are baking, buy wholemeal flour. If you find it difficult to use, try using half white and half wholemeal.
- Move over to more peas, beans and lentils. Canned beans and other kinds of pulse vegetables are easy to use because they do not require soaking and prolonged cooking.

More Fruit, Vegetables and Salads

Apart from providing fibre in your diet, these foods help to give you essential vitamins and minerals and are thought to cut the risk of heart disease and reduce blood cholesterol levels.

Less Sugar

As well as helping to increase your weight, a high sugar diet is associated with dental decay and gum disease. Sucrose, dextrose, glucose and fructose – as well as honey, syrup, raw sugar, brown sugar, cane sugar and caramel – should all be avoided where possible.

How to eat less sugar

- Buy canned fruit in juice, instead of syrup.
- Avoid frosted or honey-coated breakfast cereals.
- Cut down on sweets, chocolates, cakes and biscuits.
- Choose sugar-reduced jams, instead of standard varieties.

Alcohol

A high alcohol intake may lead to serious health problems. Since some pain is relieved by alcohol, great care must be taken not to over-indulge. It is suggested, unless you have been advised by your doctor to take less, that '*safe*' drinking levels are:

Men: 21 units per week. Women: 14 units per week.

One unit of alcohol is:-

- Half a pint of normal-strength beer or cider.
- One single measure of spirits.
- One glass of wine.

- Whatever your intake within these limits, remember to stick to the basic rules: always have alcohol with food; carefully read the labels of over-the-counter or prescribed drugs – they may advise against taking alcohol; never drink and drive.

Choosing Healthy Meals

If you embark on a diet, it is important to take into account individual food preferences, family habits and social customs. In the West we are spoilt for choice when shopping for our meals, a point for which we should be grateful. No food is truly 'junk', though if eaten in excess it may be unhealthy. If you are interested in the nutritional content of the food you buy, get into the habit of reading labels. Many of the big food chains, such as Tesco, Sainsbury and Safeway produce good leaflets on nutritional topics, including food labelling.

Suggested Meal Plan

Breakfast

Fruit or fruit juice or yoghurt.
High-fibre breakfast cereal or porridge.
Bread, toast or roll (preferably wholemeal or bran enriched).

Snack Meal

Soup (e.g. lentil).
Fish (tuna, sardine, mackerel, fish fingers etc), chicken or lean meat, baked beans, reduced fat cheese or an occasional egg.
Bread, toast or roll (preferably wholemeal), crispbread, filled jacket potato or pasta. With salad if available.
Fresh fruit, low fat yoghurt, scone or bun.

Main Meal

Soup if hungry, or fruit juice, or melon slice.
Fish, poultry or lean meat; vegetarian dish.
Potatoes, preferably boiled or baked in skins, or pasta, or rice.
Vegetables or salad.
Fruit: fresh, canned in juice or stewed; or low fat milk pudding; or low fat yoghurt; or Fromage Frais.

Bedtime

If you have a problem sleeping it may be helpful to have a milk or milk-based drink. If you are absolutely starving, have a high-fibre breakfast cereal or porridge.

Between-meal Snacks

These really should be avoided if you are seriously trying to slim or control weight. If you are desperately hungry, eat fruit or drink a cup of tea or coffee.

Daily

Include either one pint of skimmed, three-quarters of a pint of semi-skimmed or half a pint of full cream milk.

Weekly

A quarter pound of butter, or full fat margarine, or half a pound of half fat spread.

RATE YOUR DIET

FAT

Pick the foods you eat regularly at home and find the score

Food \ Score	1	2	3	Write your score here
Milk	Full fat (silver, gold, green, red top)	Semi-skimmed (red and white striped top)	Skimmed (blue and white crossed top	
Cheese	Full fat (most cheese) eg. Chedder, Stilton	Medium fat eg. Edam, Brie, Shape, Tendale, Camembert	Low fat eg. cottage	
Meat and alternatives	Fatty meat (sausages, bacon, pasties, pies) Fried fish, and meat most days	Red meat (beef pork, lamb) Nuts most days	Poultry, fish (white and oily not fried) beans, pulses most days	
Biscuits, pies pastries	Most days	Weekly	Rarely	
Butter, Margarine	Thickly spread	Thinly spread	Scraping on bread, or low fat alternative	
Fried foods and oils	Most days	Weekly	Rarely	
Eggs	Most days	Weekly	Rarely	
			Your total score	

0 - 13	Try to decrease your fat
14 - 17	Good
18 - 21	Very good

How to improve your score

Eat less:	Lower fat alternatives:
Full fat milk and yoghurt	Semi-skimmed milk and skimmed milk
Fat on meat, sausages, luncheon meat, pork pies, salamis	Low fat yogurt Poultry, lean meat, fish
High fat cheeses - cheddar, stilton, cream cheeses	Medium fat cheeses
Cream and chocolate covered biscuits	Plain unsweetened biscuits
Pies and pasties Fried foods	Grilled, poached, stewed baked foods
Butter, margerine, oils lard	Low fat spreads

SUGAR

Pick the foods you eat regularly at home and find the score

Score / Food	1	2	3	Write your score here
Sugar in drinks	Sugar in tea or coffee	Sweetner in drinks	No sugar in drinks	
Sugar in/on breakfast cereals	Sugar or honey coated cereals Sugar added to cereals at the table	Sugar in cereals eg. All-Bran, Branflakes, raisin Splits	Unsweetened cereals eg. Shredded Wheat, porridge, unsweetened muesli	
Sweets/chocolates	Most days	2 - 3 times a week	Once a week or less	
Sweet puddings	Most days	2 - 3 times a week	Once a week or less	
Biscuits	Most days	2 - 3 times a week	Once a week or less	
Fruit	Tinned in syrup	Dried fruits	Fresh fruit or tinned in natural juice	
			Your total score	

0 - 11	Try to decrease yo sugar
12 - 17	Good
18	Very good

How to improve your score

Eat less:

Sugar, sweets, chocolates
Fizzy drinks, fruit squashes and drinks
Cakes, pastries, sweet biscuits and puddings, sweetened yoghurts
Fruit tinned ih heavy syrup
Check labels for sugar, sucrose, glucose, dextrose, caramel

Lower sugar alternatives:

Fresh fruit, nuts
Pure unsweetened fruit juice, low calorie drinks
Plain biscuits, crackers, crispbreads
Fruit based desserts, flour based puddings with wholemeal flour and less sugar
Natural or low fat/low sugar yoghurts
Fruit tinned in natural juices

FIBRE

Pick the foods you eat regularly at home and find the score

Food \ Score	1	2	3	Write your score here
Breakfast cereal	Rarely or never eat, *or* sugar coated cereals eg. Sugar Smacks and Frosties	Cornflakes, Rice Krispies	Wholegrain cereals eg. Shredded Wheat, porridge unsweetened, muesli, Weetabix	
Bread	White	Brown, softgrain white	Wholemeal or high fibre white	
Potatoes, pasta	Do not eat or only rarely	Eat potatoes, white rice or pasta most days	Eat potatoes in jackets: brown rice or pasta most days	
Pulses, beans, nuts etc.	Rarely or never eaten	Less than one a week	1 - 3 times per week	
Vegetables (all kinds)	Less than once a week	Several times a week	Daily	
Fruit (fresh or dried)	Less than once a week	Several times a week	Daily	
			Your total score	

0 - 11 Try to increase your fibre
12 - 17 Good
18 Very good

How to improve your score

Eat less:
White flour and bread
White rice and pasta
Sweets, sugar

Eat more:
Wholemeal flour and bread
Brown rice and wholemeal pasta
Fruit - all kinds
Vegetables - all kinds
Beans - including baked beans and pulses

NB: Increase fibre score needs increased fluid (eg. water, low calorie squash)

REMEMBER

- Exercise daily.
- Aim for realistic goals.
- Follow a realistic exercise programme.
- You are what you eat.

5

Mastering relaxation

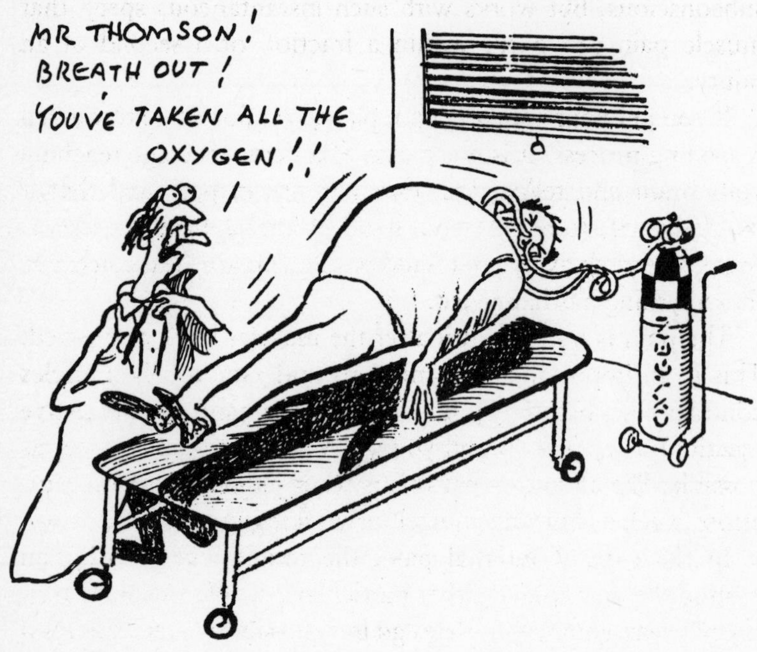

Years of pain research and the experience of hundreds of doctors working in pain management indicate that it is almost impossible to have chronic pain without having muscle spasm. No matter how relaxed you may feel, it is almost certain that you have tightness of the muscles linked to the area of pain.

Even if you believe that you do not need to learn how to relax, the physiological facts state otherwise. Pain, as we have seen, causes sufferers to lose their locus of control, allowing pain to take them over and dictate their lives. Relaxation is the trigger to regaining lost control. It is easy to learn, but requires months of patience and a determination to put time aside each day to make it work.

Pain and muscle spasms go hand in hand. The reaction of a muscle to injury or discomfort is faster than the process of thought. It does not come from the conscious, or even the subconscious, but works with such instantaneous speed that muscle pain can occur within a fraction of a second of an injury.

If you put your hand on a hot plate, you do not go through a reasoning process. It is not a case of a nerve message reaching your brain and telling you that you are in pain and that it would be wise to remove your hand. What happens in reality is that you snatch away your hand before you are even conscious that anything has happened.

The pain is not felt until after the muscles have contracted. This is an important mechanism to understand. The muscles contract even before you know you are in pain as a protective reaction. They jerk to pull you away from the pain as fast as possible. We all know that this is what happens in acute situations, such as burning yourself or pricking your finger.

In the case of internal pain, the muscles go into spasm around the area to make that particular part of your body rest. If you break your leg, muscles go into spasm to create a natural splint. Similarly with appendicitis, the muscles of the abdomen go as rigid as a board, which is one of the signs medical students are taught to look for when diagnosing it.

The patient has no control over this. Muscle spasm is a reflex reaction – but not always a useful one.

If you dislocate your shoulder an intense muscle spasm locks around it to keep it in place. Patients have to be anaesthetised to have their shoulder manipulated back into place. On many occasions, as soon as the anaesthetic has taken effect and their muscles are relaxed, the shoulder slips back into position almost of its own accord.

At times muscle spasm can be useful, but occasionally it can have no practical use whatever.

In almost every case of chronic pain, the muscle spasm accompanying it is useless. The sufferer does not want to be forced to rest. He needs to be active to overcome his pain, but muscle tension prevents this, giving rise to many problems. The pain and discomfort of needlessly tense muscles can induce anxiety, depression and make you tense as a person.

What makes this difficult for many chronic pain sufferers is that, if they have been tense for ten years, they are no longer aware of it. Many people on the Pain Management Programme adamantly claim that they have no need to learn relaxation, when their physiological signs clearly say otherwise.

In the cycle of pain, muscle tension leads to more pain, fear of future pain, fear, bad posture, lack of sleep, more muscle tension – and so it goes on.

Unless chronic pain patients unlock their muscle tension, there is every possibility of their general health becoming worse. Sitting in front of the TV or knitting does nothing to relieve reflex muscle tension. The only way to make positive progress is to learn one of the various methods of conscious relaxation and to tell your body and your subconscious exactly what you want it to do.

Chronic pain has a life of its own, even when the original illness or damage has disappeared. Chronic muscle spasms can result from an acute injury, such as tearing a muscle, injuring a nerve root or breaking a bone. Even when the original injury has healed, or the bone has mended, or the nerve has recovered, the spasm can remain. The pain continues to be generated along the same nerve pathways, but from a different cause.

Insurance companies are familiar with claims from accident

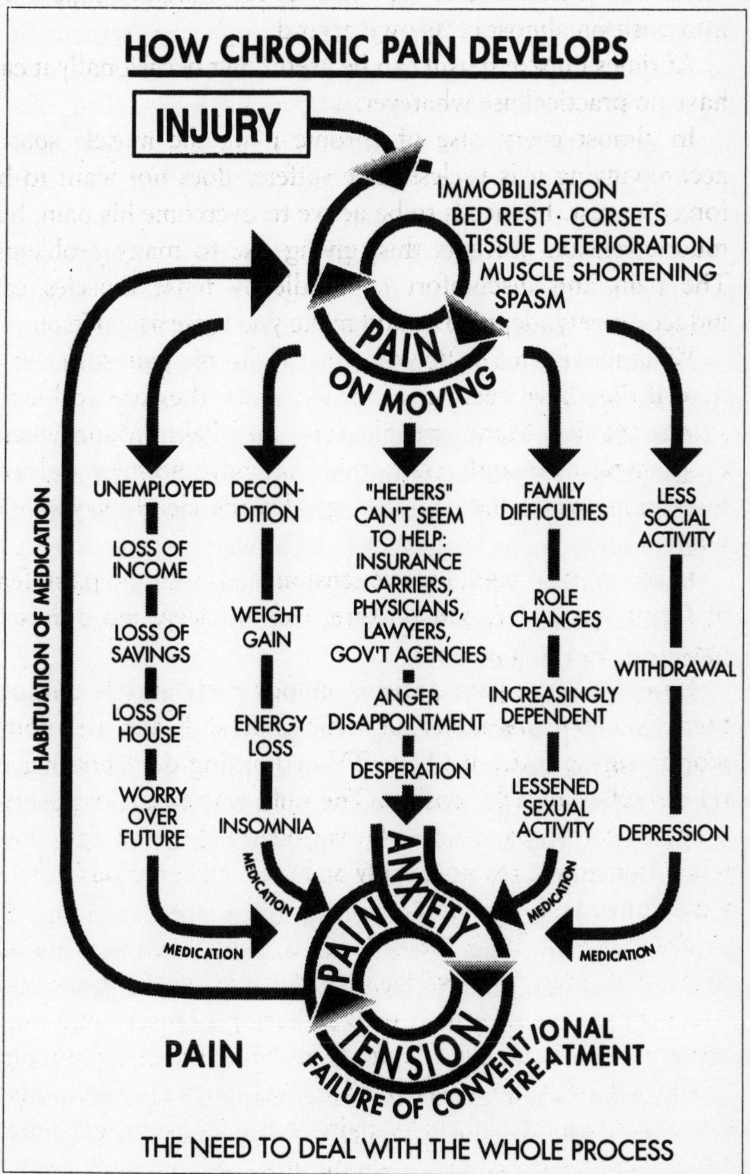
HOW CHRONIC PAIN DEVELOPS
INJURY
IMMOBILISATION
BED REST · CORSETS
TISSUE DETERIORATION
MUSCLE SHORTENING
SPASM
PAIN
ON MOVING
UNEMPLOYED
LOSS OF INCOME
LOSS OF SAVINGS
LOSS OF HOUSE
WORRY OVER FUTURE
DECON-DITION
WEIGHT GAIN
ENERGY LOSS
INSOMNIA
"HELPERS" CAN'T SEEM TO HELP: INSURANCE CARRIERS, PHYSICIANS, LAWYERS, GOV'T AGENCIES
ANGER DISAPPOINTMENT
DESPERATION
FAMILY DIFFICULTIES
ROLE CHANGES
INCREASINGLY DEPENDENT
LESSENED SEXUAL ACTIVITY
LESS SOCIAL ACTIVITY
WITHDRAWAL
DEPRESSION
HABITUATION OF MEDICATION
MEDICATION
MEDICATION
MEDICATION
MEDICATION
ANXIETY
PAIN
TENSION
PAIN
FAILURE OF CONVENTIONAL TREATMENT
THE NEED TO DEAL WITH THE WHOLE PROCESS

victims who have hurt their back at work, or suffered a whiplash injury in a car. When their doctor examines them, he can find nothing wrong, but the pain still persists. He may diagnose a muscle spasm but feels, in all fairness, that he cannot attribute it to the accident. There may no longer be anything physically wrong with the person, but the pain continues to be disabling and real.

Someone with arthritis may find that their arthritis disappears but the pain is maintained by muscle spasm. Occasionally, there may not even have been any physical disease at all – the whole problem was caused by muscle spasm in the first place.

Tension affects the muscles and organs of the body and can give rise to such alarming symptoms as headaches, pains elsewhere, sweating, insomnia, indigestion and heart palpitations, which, in turn, can increase alarm and anxiety.

A tense muscle is a painful one. It limits and restricts your movement, makes you feel tired, irritable and unable to concentrate or think clearly.

Relaxation is the opposite of tension – a method of exercise which can help you overcome the physical and emotional suffering of the agony of muscle tension. It is a skill and, as with all skills, practice makes perfect. Once you have learned the technique, you can relax anytime, anywhere and ease the pressure on your body and mind.

The difficult aspect is that relaxation is not like riding a bicycle. Once you have learned it, it does not come automatically. It is important to be aware of some of the problems and remember them at times when you feel that your progress is slow.

Relaxation is not easy, but some people pick it up more effortlessly than others. The advice from anyone who practises relaxation regularly is to stick with it – the benefits can literally change your life.

Relaxation:

- Relieves the spasm of a muscle.
- Releases endorphins to relieve pain.
- Helps you regain your locus of control. If you can learn to relax and reduce your pain, even to a small degree, you are in control again.

Once you can control your pain it assumes a totally different perspective. It no longer controls *you* and confidence takes over from fear and anxiety. On occasions, there have been patients who have mastered the art of relaxation and no longer need to put it into practice; the knowledge that they can control their own muscles is sufficient to keep their pain at a reduced level. For them, it has provided a feeling of security, rather like carrying a spare tyre in your car. If you know you have one, the prospect of a puncture poses no worry. If you have no means of dealing with it, then the thought preoccupies you and assumes an importance that it does not deserve.

Which is the best method of relaxation to select?

All have advantages and disadvantages and the devotees of one method may criticise another. The technique with the greatest chance of success is the one which feels most comfortable to you. There are many: meditation, hypnosis, yoga, T'ai Chi, the tense-and-relax method, visualisation.

Preference may depend on many things. Some cultures already have disciplines which tend to draw them to relaxation naturally. Yoga is an accepted part of the Indian lifestyle; millions of Chinese practice T'ai Chi in their local park each morning; Muslims pray five times every day. All of these combine physical movement and focusing the mind.

In the West, traditional safety mechanisms have been

eroded. Church attendances have declined, the friendly corner chemist who would listen to your troubles and 'mix a good bottle' has been replaced by self-service drug stores. Even the opportunity to share problems in a doorstep chat with a neighbour has become less common. By turing to drugs and doctors instead, we have lost something of the art of unloading tension. Relaxation does not come easy, so it is important to find a way of achieving it that feels comfortable to you.

'The technique most useful for someone learning to relax is Progressive Muscular Relaxation,' says neuropsychologist Dr Eric Ghadiali. 'The principle is that you focus progressively on each muscle group of the body, first tensing as hard as you can and noticing what it actually feels like when it is tensed, then letting go and relaxing and experiencing how it feels for that particular muscle group to be relaxed.

'Sometimes, when people have particular pain conditions, tensing the muscle may bring on the pain. If that is the case, the advice is simply not to tense that particular muscle.

'The advantage of the technique is that it is easy. It is also recognised as one of the quickest ways of teaching people how to relax by increasing your awareness of when you become tense and how you are when relaxed.

'The other main method is Autogenic Training, when you direct your attention to different muscles groups and concentrate on relaxing thoughts. Instead of thinking how much pain you have, how bad it feels and how awful things are, you focus on a particular muscle instead. Your thoughts are that it is feeling very heavy, very comfortable, very loose, very limp. By doing this progressively – moving from one muscle group to the next – you will be able to relax yourself.

'One of the difficulties people encounter is that they cannot concentrate. The pain becomes too intrusive and takes their attention away. They may even be worried about making dinner, or what time their partner is arriving home from work.

The message here is to stick with it. Keep trying to relax, even though you may not feel better in the early stages. Remember that it is a skill and you will gradually improve.'

From his experience, Dr Ghadiali advises creating a daily relaxation routine:

- Put aside half an hour each day to devote to relaxation.
- Tell your family and friends what you are doing so they do not interrupt you. Once they know how serious you are, they will provide valuable encouragement and support.
- Choose the same bed, mat or chair each day for your relaxation. A routine helps to set your mind and put you in a more relaxed state for the exercise.

Coping with pain requires a different lifestyle and new routines, jettisoning old, unhelpful habits and acquiring new ones which encourage positive progress.

When you are sitting or lying comfortably it is important to breathe properly in a calm way. Be careful not to breathe too deeply – taking very deep breaths can sometimes make you feel a little more tense.

The method taught on the Pain Management Programme is to sit or lie with a straight spine. After a full exhalation, inhale through your nose while counting slowly to four. As you inhale, first fill the lower section of your lungs. Your diaphragm will push your abdomen outward, to make room for the air.

Then, fill the middle part of your lungs as your lower ribs and chest move forward to accommodate more air. Next, fill the upper part of your lungs. As you raise your chest and shoulders slightly, draw in your abdomen a little to support your lungs. With practice, these three steps can be performed in one smooth, continuous operation.

Hold your breath for a slow count of three. Exhale through your mouth, making a relaxing, whooshing sound, like wind, as you blow out to a slow count of four.

As you exhale, follow the same pattern as the inhalation. Pull your abdomen in, then exhale from your middle chest. Finally, exhale from your upper chest as you allow your shoulders to sink and relax and your abdomen to puff out again slightly.

Not everyone is a natural 'belly breather' and the rhythm may be difficult for you to get into. It may help while learning to place one hand lightly on your chest and the other on your abdomen to feel them rise and fall as you inhale and exhale. As the sequence becomes automatic, you can return your hands to a more comfortable position. Scan your body for areas of tension, and return to the sound and flow of your breathing as you become more and more relaxed.

Continue this for five minutes. If you become light-headed at any time, alternate six regular breaths with six deep breaths. Once you have learned the breathing exercise, you can practice it whenever you feel yourself becoming tense.

Always try to begin your relaxation session with breathing exercises to put yourself in a calm frame of mind. The important thing is to breath gently and regularly, feeling your body relax in the process.

PROGRESSIVE MUSCLE RELAXATION

These simple exercises, which take about 20 minutes, will help you cope with your pain more effectively. They are based on widely used and well-established techniques that are known to help people relax more effectively. Learning how to relax is like learning any new skill – the more you practise, the better you become. Initially, it is recommended that you try these exercises at least every day, more often if you can manage it. Don't worry if you find it difficult at first, or don't seem to be succeeding. The trick is not to try too hard.

The exercises you are about to go through will help you to relax all the muscles in your body. They involve repetition, but the rhythm created is part of the beneficial process. During the session you will be progressively tensing, then relaxing all your muscles. While you are doing this, concentrate on the difference between tension and relaxation.

It is obviously impossible to do these exercises by constantly consulting the book. Either get someone to read them to you – it is good for a friend or family member to take part – or, if no one is available, read them into a tape recorder and play them back. Alternatively, use the relaxation tape 'Coping With Pain' from the Pain Relief Foundation. (Details can be found in the back of the book.)

Method:

First, close your eyes. Concentrate on the sound of your breathing. Breathe slowly and regularly, not too deeply. Begin to notice how every time you breathe out you gradually begin to feel more relaxed and more comfortable.

1 Start by concentrating on the muscles in your hands, wrists and lower arms. You can tense these by squeezing your hands into fists. Now clench your fists and feel the tension in the muscles. Clench them tight – feel the tension. Tighter – and relax.

Relax the muscles and let go of the tension. Enjoy the feeling of letting go. Notice the difference between tension and relaxation. How the muscles in your hands and your lower arms feel very loose, very limp, very relaxed.

tense these by biting your teeth together and clenching your jaws. Clamp your teeth together and feel the tension build in your mouth and jaw. Hold it, feel the pressure and relax.

Let your teeth part slightly and you will notice the difference between tension and relaxation as the muscles in your jaw and mouth go loose and limp. As you become more and more deeply relaxed, so you become more comfortable.

Notice now how all the muscles in your lips, face and forehead feel very smooth, heavy and comfortable. Your arms feel very heavy, limp and relaxed. You are breathing slowly and regularly. Every time you breathe out, you feel a greater sense of well-being and comfort.

9 And now the muscles in your chest. These can be tensed by breathing in as deeply as you can. Fill your lungs, breathe very deeply and hold it. Feel the tension in your chest increase and the muscles in your chest become tense. Hold it until it begins to feel uncomfortable – and relax.

Feel all the muscles in your chest relax as you breathe out. Continue breathing normally. Not too deeply, but regularly and evenly. Notice the feeling in your chest and the difference between tension and relaxation. The muscles in your chest now feel very comfortable and relaxed.

10 Now focus on the muscles in your stomach. You can tense these by pulling your stomach in tightly, as if preparing to receive a blow. Make your stomach as tight and tense as you can. Feel the tension tightening. Hold it – and relax.

Let go of all the tension in your stomach muscles. Notice how they feel very loose, comfortable and deeply relaxed.

11 Now the muscles in your legs. You can tense these by stretching your legs out in front of you, making them stiff and straight and pointing your toes away from your head. Stretch your legs in front of you and make them as tight and rigid as you can by pointing your toes. Feel the tension throughout your legs. Tighten all the muscles – tighter – and relax.

Let your legs and feet return to a comfortable position. Notice the difference between tension and relaxation in all the muscles of your legs and feet and the way they now feel very heavy, very loose and deeply relaxed.

All the muscles in your body now feel very limp and comfortable. Your whole body feels heavier as you feel yourself sinking deeper into the chair or bed that you are lying on. As you sink deeper, you become more relaxed and comfortable.

Your legs are heavy and deeply relaxed. Your hands and arms are very loose. All the muscles in your chest and stomach are very limp and relaxed. The muscles in your forehead, your face, your lips and mouth are very loose and comfortable.

Spend the next few moments focusing on how pleasant and comfortable you feel. You may find it helpful to imagine a relaxing scene or an idyllic scene from your past – perhaps sitting in a warm, sunny garden or lying on a beach listening to the sound of the waves.

Finish the exercise by counting backwards from four to one. As you open your eyes you will feel more refreshed and alert while remaining comfortable and relaxed. As you keep up with exercises, you will find yourself generally more interested in what you are doing, calmer, more settled, more confident to do what you want to do and much more in control of your pain.

As you become more accomplished at relaxation, you can use the time at the end of an exercise to plan how to cope with things that might arise during the day. Practice this while going about your daily activities, so that no muscle tension creeps in to give you pain afterwards.

AN ALTERNATIVE METHOD

Breathing

Try to achieve a slow and steady breathing pattern. Breathe using your diaphragm. The top part of your chest should stay fairly still and your stomach should slowly rise as you breathe in and fall as you breathe out.

Face

(i) Raise your eyebrows, hold, lower them.
(ii) Push your eyebrows towards your nose, hold, release them.
(iii) Clench your lips and teeth together tightly, hold, then release.
(iv) Check that your tongue is not pressed hard against the roof of your mouth.

Neck

(i) Press your head down into the pillow, hold and release. Let your head rest gently on the pillow.
(ii) Raise your head slightly off the pillow, hold and release.

Shoulders

(i) Push your shoulders up towards your ears, hold and release. Notice how they fall into a lower position.

Arms

(i) Lift your arms half an inch off the floor. Make your elbows straight. Hold and release.

(ii) Leaving your arms supported on the mat, spread your fingers out away from you. Hold and release.

Stomach

(i) Pull your stomach in towards you, hold and release. Notice how difficult breathing is when your stomach is tense.

Bottom

(i) Clench your cheeks together tightly. Feel your bottom lift slightly off the floor, hold and then release.

Legs

(i) Push your ankles and toes down, away from your body. Make your knees straight. Hold and release.

(ii) Let your hips and knees roll out slightly and your feet flop to the side (like ten minutes to two on the hands of a clock).

(iii) Pull your ankles and toes in towards you, hold and release.

Your body may feel quite heavy now and you should feel calm and at ease. Lie there, savouring the sensation, and notice the difference between how tense you were previously and the way you feel at present. This quick relaxation technique should be used to supplement the longer method previously described, not instead of it. It could be done, for instance, just before or just after doing your physical exercise routine.

Relaxation is about regaining control through a new awareness of your body, but not all tension is caused by muscle spasm. There can be many other sources of tension in life that arise as secondary consequences of pain.

'Pain makes people irritable,' says Dr Ghadiali. 'It makes them bad tempered; stops them mixing with their family and friends; it makes them ratty. When people are like that, these bad feelings can sometimes be infectious and make the whole family feel uptight – and that can be an additional source of stress.

'If you can avoid these effects or deal with them in a different way, you can reduce your tension. If you don't recognise them or deal with them, they will still be there, building additional tension.

'These exercises might take 20 minutes, so when you devote half an hour a day to relaxation, try to spend the rest of the time thinking ahead to how you respond to stressful situations with that build-up of tension. Some people clench their teeth when they are in an argument or het-up, for example. In a traffic jam they clench their hands or hunch their shoulders when driving. Try to become more aware of how tense you are in everyday situations.

'Then, instead of responding in the usual way, you can respond by breathing properly and applying your relaxation techniques.

'The secret is increased awareness. In a way, you are conditioning yourself. When you are tense in certain situations, the idea is to decondition yourself and break the association between stressful situations and feeling tense and so replace the tension with a relaxed reaction.'

Many chronic pain patients find relaxation a difficult knack to learn because they do not know what they are looking for. Some have no idea what a relaxed muscle feels like and have no yardstick to compare it to. When they do begin to acquire relaxation skills, it is usually sitting in a comfortable chair or lying on a mat.

If you have, say, a whiplash injury and are frightened of getting behind the wheel of your car again, then putting relaxation into practice is a different proposition to listening to a soothing tape in an armchair. You must be prepared to broaden your relaxation methods and apply different techniques to your own particular problem. You may have to sit at home and visualize situations: driving in heavy traffic, turning from left to right, shifting the gears and learn to relax your muscles in all these situations before embarking on them. Eventually, you need to be able to relax even in the most stressful situations, such as driving in traffic jams when late or being told unpleasant news.

If you really want to be active again, these are the levels you should aim for. They may take six months or even two years to achieve but, if you are prepared to put in the time and effort, the results are worth it.

One patient ran a family hotel in North Wales. She had had a slipped disc, which had been successfully treated, but she continued to suffer pain from muscle spasm. Because of her disability, she had to employ three additional staff to continue her work in the hotel.

On the course, she worked hard and had the right positive attitude, but failed to make much progress. Despite taking all the ideas on board, she returned to the clinic to complain that she was still in pain. Her back muscles were still locked in spasm and we knew only relaxation could be of any benefit.

She had learned the technique on the Pain Management Programme, but had been able to make little progress. She went back to the hotel and continued to practise relaxation every day. After a while, she reported some improvement; she was now able to walk around more, but still could not undertake difficult jobs, such as making the beds.

Four and a half years later, after persisting every day, she mastered the knack of relaxing her muscles at will and relieving the pain. 'Most of my pain has gone away,' she wrote triumphantly. 'I still get pain when I try to do things, but I can handle it. My greatest joy has been learning to relax my back muscles. It has enabled me to work again.'

Through practice she achieved a new awareness of herself which enabled her to cope with her pain. No matter how long it may take you to acquire the skill, whether it be weeks or years, the freedom it rewards you with repays the effort.

Chronic pain causes all kinds of psychological distress, leading to a vicious cycle of tension and more pain. Relaxation techniques are a helpful way of breaking the cycle and reducing tension pain.

Margaret, a recent patient, suffered chronic back pain for 30 years before learning to control it. She says:

> 'The therapy, medical advice and a new way of facing pain mentally have all helped me tremendously. The Pain Programme has been rewarding because it has given me a different attitude to my pain. Most of all, the relaxation and exercises have been very important. I had been very inactive, sitting and resting a lot when the pain in my back became unrelenting. I have since learned that this is not the thing to do.'

There are times when it may take a great effort to put the time aside for relaxation, you may find concentration difficult, pain demands your attention or depletes your energy. No matter how low you feel, always try to make the effort. The close link between body and mind means that the very motion of preparing yourself for relaxation and going through the exercise will affect your outlook and improve your sense of well-being. The response to pain and its associated problems of tension and depression is to do something. The framework and routine of relaxation and exercise provide a reliable, positive method of making progress towards conquering your pain. Determination to reclaim your life and never again allow pain to conquer you is the strongest weapon in your armoury.

REMEMBER

- Daily relaxation - 30 minutes of the method of your choice.
- Visualize different situations at the end of the exercise and how you might cope.
- Remember your internal locus of control - 'I am in control here'.
- Think positively about the future - I *will* be able to do this.'

6

Thinking, feeling, doing

Pain, as we have seen, is about receiving messages. Most kinds of pain contain a physical element, a signal sent out from within the body warning that something is wrong. The brain acts as a radio receiver with an emergency frequency constantly open, listening out for distress messages.

Everyone tunes in to his or her pain frequency differently. Some people have the volume turned down low because they are not expecting anything, others have it high because they are always anticipating trouble.

The system works rather like the yachtsman who takes his boat out for the weekend. Once at sea, he turns on his short-wave radio and leaves it tuned to the coastguard channel. If the weather is calm and he is sunning himself on deck, he will probably have the volume low because the chance of any warnings being transmitted is slight. If a storm is expected, he will have his receiver on full volume, alert for emergency and distress messages.

Pain has two major aspects – the physical and psychological. The psychological, or mental, side does not cause pain, but acts as a volume control, turning the intensity up or down. Like the yachtsman, when the volume is high you receive a stronger blast of distress message. On a personal level, there is no good reason to receive these amplified, distorted signals as chronic pain performs no useful purpose.

The more effort you make to understand how you react to pain, the easier it is to learn how to turn the pain volume down and generally feel better.

There are two important reasons why some people suffer more pain than others. Firstly, their volume control is permanently turned high because they are expecting pain. If you have been in daily pain for, say, 20 years, then it is understandable that you wake up in the morning waiting for it to happen. Secondly, because the psychological factors which turn up the pain volume are part of your individual make-up.

People who keep their pain volume turned down receive only weak signals. Listening out for warning calls does not greatly occupy their attention. They are not on alert, straining for the first indication of trouble but, more than likely, preoccupied in doing or thinking about other things. After a while, they do not even pick up some of the messages being transmitted.

Those who have acquired the knack of turning down their pain volume are basically no different to others who feel more pain. The only thing which sets them apart is their attitude. As they have discovered more about themselves and what makes them tick psychologically, their outlook on pain has become more realistic.

If, however, you have become a pain-watcher – focusing your attention on pain all the time; allowing it to dominate your life; if you wake in the morning and check immediately for pain; if you stop working, stop mixing with people; spend all your time visiting doctors or searching for someone to help you with your pain, then it will become worse as the psychological volume is turned up. Once you find ways of allocating less importance to pain – putting your mind on other things, taking up interests, mixing socially and becoming active – then pain messages will inevitably become weaker and weaker.

It is rather like the problem encountered in an office block which had only four lifts in the lobby. They were hopelessly inadequate to take the hundreds of office workers who used them. The lifts were always overcrowded and tempers frayed as people waited. Arguments broke out and staff held angry protest meetings. The owners of the building were in a dilemma because there was no space to install more lifts.

As business increased, staff became late for appointments and frustration rose. In desperation, the company brought in a consultant who devised a simple answer. He lined the entire lobby with mirrors. Staff became so distracted looking at themselves and others that they forgot completely about their problems. Replacing unproductive thoughts about pain can have a similar effect in reducing the negative emotions which accompany them.

Problems arise when you become so preoccupied with pain

that it distorts your thinking. Your perception of pain becomes unrealistic. Allkinds of worries stream through your mind – the pain is much more serious than people imagine, your doctor has overlooked or misunderstood your condition, your health is probably much worse than you have been led to believe. Thoughts like these lead to catastrophizing – fanning the flames with exaggerated anxieties and fears.

Negative thoughts nurture negative emotions which, in turn, lead to negative behaviour. The story of the businessman who had a bout of indigestion while recovering from an ulcer (see page 34) is a classic example of the domino effect of thoughts, feelings and behaviour running out of control. His catastrophizing and unrealistic view of what was happening turned a mild tummy disorder into another, very real, ulcer.

When you suffer chronic pain, particularly if you have had it for many years, it is important to work towards a cooler, more rational understanding of your condition, placing your pain more firmly in perspective. The way you address your pain and cope with it stems from how you address yourself. Psychologists call these negative internal conversations *cognitive distortions.*

The suffering which you put down to your pain is, in fact, the result of a number of factors. Two of the most important are:

- distress about the effects pain has on your life and daily activities.
- worries about its meaning and implications.

Your thoughts are not just a running commentary on everything you see, hear and feel. They can be an active ingredient contributing to worry and unhappiness. Past experiences, beliefs and assumptions all jostle to take over the driving seat when your thoughts run away with you.

If, for example, you secretly believe that your pain is caused by a serious disease which no one has detected, then you may quickly imagine it becoming worse, visualize a bleak future, brood on how neglected you feel or how angry you are about the doctors who supposedly overlooked it – it isn't difficult to imagine what that does to your pain gates!

Thoughts such as these can lower your mood and make you feel hopeless about coping with pain, even make you determined to find a doctor who will do something drastic to take it all away, but none of them will help. Pat, a 44-year-old housewife, later looked back on the confusion into which pain had plunged her: 'I imagined I had every disease under the sun,' she said. 'I was convinced everyone was hiding the awful truth from me.'

Sadly, there are occasions when it may be too late to reverse this. Many years ago, Linda, a beautician, went to her doctor with backache. He examined her and sent her for further examinations for ankylosing spondylitis. When she was told what the examinations were for, she jumped to the conclusion that she had the disease. Later, the doctors discussed among themselves the fact that she did not have it but, unfortunately, someone neglected to tell her.

Linda went on thinking that this painful and progressive condition was becoming worse until she enrolled on the Pain Management Programme. When we told her that she did not have any terrible underlying condition, she was too stunned and shocked to believe it. She had become so convinced that she really had a severe disease that she believed the staff were keeping something from her. As a result, she was unable to make any progress in overcoming her pain.

Runaway thoughts, or cognitive distortions, stem from an unrealistic picture of your problems. They are not part of your imagination, but ways of thinking and describing things too harshly to yourself and not taking a balanced view. Given the opportunity, underlying beliefs can interpret almost anything as basically bad. ('Is this book trying to say that I don't even think right? I really must be in a hopeless mess.') By studying yourself you can learn to test these thoughts against what is really happening and change them. Worry is usually about dwelling on a threat which is not present, not important and often something you can learn to cope with.

Here are some of the ways psychologists identify thinking which leads to unnecessary worry and anxiety:

Selective attention to possible threatening signs, rather than giving your attention to more harmless indicators. For example, worrying that the doctor has asked for another X-ray, rather than accepting his reassurance that the investigation has been satisfactory so far.

A classic case concerned a nine-year-old boy who came round from anaesthetic after having his kidney removed. As he lay in the recovery room with his hands over the bedclothes, the surgeon asked how he felt.

The boy was relaxed and replied that he felt fine. When the surgeon left the room, the nurse asked the boy if he was worried about anything. At this point he began to cry and confessed that he was afraid of having his kidney removed. When the nurse assured him that the operation was over, he checked by slipping his hands beneath the bedclothes to feel his bandages. As soon as he realized what had happened, he immediately began to complain of pain.

Interpreting ambiguous signs as threatening. Deciding, for instance, that feeling weak must mean that something is wrong in the nervous system, rather than being caused by under-using your muscles.

Selective recall of dangerous possibilities and events which leads to over-estimating the likelihood of them occurring. Reading a chest pain as a possible heart attack rather than, say, indigestion.

Anticipation of negative outcomes and looking for ways of escape. For example: 'If I go to the cinema, my back is sure to hurt. People will notice and think I'm fussing. It will spoil the evening for my friends, so I may as well not go.'

Catastrophizing, or making a disaster out of a problem: 'It's hurting again . . . I'm no better after all this treatment . . . There must be something really wrong for it to hurt so much . . . All this effort is for nothing . . . I don't know how I can get home with all this pain . . . I'm going to crack up if this doesn't stop . . . I'll have to go home for my pain killers . . .'

When you begin to study yourself, these negative thoughts can be changed by interrupting them and developing positive alternatives: 'I can cope . . . I'm uncomfortable here, but I can control it . . . I'll be all right if I keep breathing and walk steady . . . I've handled it without panicking – that shows I can do it better . . . Now I've dealt with a few bad times it should be easier . . . If I go to the cinema I'd better sit at the end of the row then, if my back hurts, I can get up and stand at the back for a bit; maybe do a few stretches which will help, and then sit down again; my friends won't be bothered by that.'

There is a different tone to these statements. They are all positive but refer to coping with challenge or difficulty, rather than mastering it. Experience and research has shown that acknowledging the problem is more effective than trying to completely ignore it.

A mastery statement would be: '*The pain is no problem. I can work as well as I ever could.*'

A coping statement would sound like: '*Although the pain makes it harder to work, I feel better if I keep going at a steady rate.*'

The message here is that mastery statements set you up to fail and are not a realistic way to cope with pain, whereas coping statements are more positive and can be proved right. A patient called Pat ended his goodbye speech with the words: '*I am now very hopeful that, although I may still have my pain, I am going to have a better quality of life and try to enjoy it to the full.*' Everyone felt that Pat's realistic attitude to coping would help him to make good progress in overcoming his pain.

Confidence plays a central part in managing your pain. It is about realistic evaluations of situations and the resources with which you face them. If you over-estimate the difficulty of a situation, or under-estimate your ability to manage it, you tip the scales against coping in a satisfactory way.

However, when you prepare for difficulty and free yourself of failure thoughts and panic thoughts, you are much more likely to succeed. If success does not come immediately, do not feel daunted. You will be in a better position to analyse and learn from your efforts and build a base from which to move forward, working systematically towards success.

Feelings are just as important as thoughts in determining how much pain you experience. Once pain dominates your thoughts and actions, it can quickly make you unhappy and depressed. You come to feel socially isolated from other people, with pain acting almost as an invisible barrier between you and the rest of the world.

It may make you feel irritable and difficult to live with, or guilty and upset because you can no longer do the things you used to do. Relationships within the family may become more difficult and strained. It may lead you to give up work, causing financial problems which make things worse. You may feel useless and become more and more dependent on other people. As you do less and less for yourself you may become gradually more and more ruled by pain. As you feel less in control, these emotional factors add to existing problems caused by the pain.

A GP described a woman patient who developed severe chest pains on discovering a small lump in her breast. The lump was found to be harmless and, when she was reassured, the pain subsided. Extreme emotions, such as fear and anxiety, can heighten the experience of pain, while the power of suggestion has the ability to lower the volume control.

In the 1950s, an American research team led by Prof. Beecher of Boston made an interesting discovery. They studied a group of patients with severe pain who were going to be treated with morphine. Without explaining the experiment, they substituted the drug with a simple inactive sugar pill (a placebo) and found that about 35 per cent of those patients reported a marked improvement in their pain. The figure was particularly remarkable as morphine itself is effective in only about 75 per cent of cases.

Staff caring for them did not know whether they were administering morphine or a placebo. They were, however, very encouraging and optimistic, instilling a positive attitude in their patients. Reducing their anxiety and thinking positively in this way, without the use of active drugs, proved extremely effective.

A few years earlier, a similar experiment was carried out on patients suffering from severe headaches, resulting in 52 per cent reporting noticeable improvement.

The power of suggestion is also reflected in the success rate of hypnosis in pain treatment. The ability to change your outlook and attitude is a key to achieving positive results. Trying to cope with emotional aspects of pain means trying to change what you think and do in response to pain. One of the important starting points is not to think about pain, or dwell on it, any more than is necessary. The more you can divert your mind into other interests and activities, the more you will find it possible to distract yourself from pain and the less intense it will feel. Most of us have experienced a small injury or cut that only began to hurt when we noticed it. Some people are able to train their minds to almost switch off pain by relaxing or concentrating their thoughts in certain ways.

Taking a fresh look at yourself and how you react to pain is central to the learning process which helps you onto the road to a vital, active life again. Negative thoughts lead to distress and your unhappy state of mind will only be prolonged by new distortions that arise. Here are some more characteristic distortions pain sufferers experience:

Over-generalization. You give up in the middle of a task, thinking 'I never manage to finish anything.'

Emotional reasoning – taking your emotions as evidence. For example: 'I feel hopeless about my pain getting better, so there can't be anything which will help me.'

All-or-nothing thinking which channels your abilities in a negative direction. 'I didn't manage my goal of five minutes on the exercise bike on Monday – it's obviously useless bothering to exercise at all.'

Selective abstraction – when only the negative sides of a situation are taken in and remembered. Positive ones are discounted or forgotten, especially after achieving an important target: 'Okay, I got to the supermarket and did the shopping, but I only managed it because it wasn't crowded. It took me a long time and my back hurt at the end of it. I can't just go anytime like I used to.'

Arbitrary inference – another way of referring to the way you interpret things to reinforce your negative self-image. For example: 'The only reason people are nice to me is that they feel sorry for me because I'm obviously such a failure.'

Distortions such as these make it harder to manage pain. Getting life back into perspective helps you not only to plan and succeed, but to enjoy the success you have earned. The attitudes and beliefs of more than 300 chronic pain patients attending the Pain Clinic were carefully studied to find out how people coped psychologically with chronic pain. It was found that, although all patients had about the same amount of pain, those patients who had a positive attitude and a more active approach tended to cope better than patients with a more negative or passive attitude.

Measuring pain is not an easy business because of its subjective nature, nor is it a good idea for an individual to become too preoccupied with charting and recording it. However, if you are working on ways of reducing your pain levels, it is sometimes useful to record what progress you have made. There is a simple method for keeping a rough track of how your pain changes, known as the Visual Analogue Scale. This, it should be said, is a very personal indicator and not a method of comparing one person's pain with another.

Take a piece of paper and draw a horizontal line, about 10 centimetres long. A 'round figure' measurement is ideal so that you can calibrate the line with a ruler to keep a more accurate record. One end of the line represents no pain at all, while the other indicates the worst possible pain you can imagine:

NO PAIN |————————————| **WORST PAIN EVER**

If you mark the line every day at a point which you think corresponds to the amount of pain you are suffering, and measure it with a ruler, you can keep track of how your pain changes on different days according to how you are working to reduce it.

So how do you know how well you are coping with pain?

We know that how we cope depends on whether the pain volume is turned up or down by thoughts, feelings and what we do. One way of gauging our inner state is by taking note of how we express thoughts and emotions in terms of language.

Pain is a country of the mind and, like any country, has its own language. Ronald Melzack, a Professor of Psychology at McGill University in Canada devised a questionnaire which is used internationally for measuring pain more accurately. You can use it yourself to obtain a general indication of how well you are coping.

The McGill Questionnaire contains groups of words which each describe a particular type of pain. Patients attending pain clinics are asked to choose the one that best describes the way they feel. If the words in one or more groups do not fit the pain, the patient does not select any in that group or groups.

Only those that completely match what the patient is suffering are chosen. You are using it here for a slightly different purpose, but the method of picking the word-group most appropriate to you is the same.

Fill this questionnaire in now, concerning your pain, before reading on:

Look carefully at the twenty groups of words. *If* any word in the group applies to *your* pain, please circle that word – but *do not circle more than one word in any one group.* If more than one word in a group applies to your pain, you should circle *only the most suitable word* in that group.

In groups that *do not apply* to your pain, there is no need to circle any word – just leave them unmarked.

McGill-Melzack Pain Questionnaire

1
Flickering
Quivering
Pulsing
Throbbing
Beating
Pounding

2
Jumping
Flashing
Shooting

3
Pricking
Boring
Drilling
Stabbing
Lancinating

4
Sharp
Cutting
Lacerating

5
Pinching
Pressing
Gnawing
Cramping
Crushing

6
Tugging
Pulling
Wrenching

7
Hot
Burning
Scalding
Searing

8
Tingling
Itchy
Smarting
Stinging

9
Dull
Sore
Hurting
Aching
Heavy

10
Tender
Taut
Rasping
Splitting

11
Tiring
Exhausting

12
Sickening
Suffocating

13
Fearful
Frightful
Terrifying

14
Punishing
Gruelling
Cruel
Vicious
Killing

15
Wretched
Binding

16
Annoying
Troublesome
Miserable
Intense
Unbearable

17
Spreading
Radiating
Penetrating
Piercing

18
Tight
Numb
Drawing
Squeezing
Tearing

19
Cool
Cold
Freezing

20
Nagging
Nauseating
Agonizing
Dreadful
Torturing

The McGill questionnaire recognises that pain consists of different dimensions. Answers indicate both the sensory and emotional aspects of pain, which vary in different people at different times. Pain sufferers use words that show how much emotional distress is associated with their problem. If, for example, you ask someone what their pain is like, they may say: 'It's horrible,' or 'It's miserable,' 'It's wearing, depressing, frustrating,' or 'It gets me down.' These are all terms which describe the effects of pain, rather than the pain itself.

Other people might choose words which describe the sensory aspects of pain: 'It's a sharp pain', 'A stabbing pain', 'A tingling pain', 'A hot, burning pain'. If you study the language, or vocabulary, of pain carefully there are clues as to which aspect you are talking about. The word-groups you have chosen give an insight into how much pain has begun to dominate your life in terms of psychological distress. Generally, when you are coping well with your pain you are aware of its physical sensation, but do not feel that it is controlling your life. You feel on top of it and are not threatened, miserable or depressed. When you describe your pain, it is in terms of how it feels physically.

If you are not managing to cope too well, the pain is overbearing and you feel worn down. It depresses you and you tend to use emotional words to describe it. Examining the word groups you have chosen is a broad indicator of the psychological balance you are managing to achieve.

The further down the group you go, the more relevant it becomes to the interpretation of your pain. That is, if you fill in the first word in a group, it is not as significant as if you fill in the middle word and this, in turn, is not as significant as if you fill in the last word.

Human beings, of course, are not always so straightforward and compartmentalized. Some people may describe a stabbing, shooting pain in physical terms, but still feel that it has taken over their life. A rule of thumb is that if you can accept your pain and come to terms with it, then it is likely to be physical pain.

If you find it unbearable, then the time has come to examine the psychological causes. If you do not, then it is unlikely to improve.

Look particularly at word groups 11, 12, 13, 14, 15, 16 and 20. If you have circled these more than any others, pain is causing you psychological distress which you need to address. The further down these word groups you go, the worse is your psychological distress. Thus, if the pain is 'terrifying', 'killing' and 'unbearable', rather than 'fearful' and 'annoying', or 'torturing' rather than 'nagging', this indicates more distress.

While the Visual Analogue Scale provides a sum total for your whole experience of pain, the McGill Questionnaire gives a deeper indication of how much mental distress it is causing. To discover more about yourself in relation to your problems, there are more questions you can answer. Questionnaires are a good way to guide you through this because pain often alters the way you look at things.

When pain distorts your ability to reason clearly it is not easy to observe yourself in a detached way. Dr Eric Ghadiali devised a questionnaire for patients attending the Pain Relief Programme which helps to overcome this problem.

Circle the appropriate word to indicate how much you agree or disagree with the following statements. The numbers beneath each question can be added up later to calculate your score. It is important to answer all the questions.

Pain Coping Indicator

1) I feel happy about my life in general.

strongly disagree   disagree   uncertain   agree   strongly agree

2) I have lost my confidence.

strongly disagree   disagree   uncertain   agree   strongly agree

3) I try to avoid other people when I have pain.

strongly disagree   disagree   uncertain   agree   strongly agree

4) I feel my pain cuts me off from other people.

strongly disagree   disagree   uncertain   agree   strongly agree

5) I sometimes worry that I have a serious illness.

strongly disagree   disagree   uncertain   agree   strongly agree

6) My pain affects the way I get on with family and friends a great deal.

strongly disagree   disagree   uncertain   agree   strongly agree

7) My pain makes me feel tense and frustrated.

strongly disagree   disagree   uncertain   agree   strongly agree

8) My pain makes me feel miserable most of the time.

strongly disagree	disagree	uncertain	agree	strongly agree

9) I have to rely on other people a great deal because of my pain.

strongly disagree	disagree	uncertain	agree	strongly agree

10) I never go out because people do not want to know you when you have pain.

strongly disagree	disagree	uncertain	agree	strongly agree

11) My pain stops me from leading a normal life.

strongly disagree	disagree	uncertain	agree	strongly agree

12) I find it very difficult to relax.

strongly disagree	disagree	uncertain	agree	strongly agree

13) My pain makes me opt out of things.

strongly disagree	disagree	uncertain	agree	strongly agree

14) My pain stops me going places.

strongly disagree	disagree	uncertain	agree	strongly agree

15) My pain makes it difficult to socialize with people.

strongly disagree | disagree | uncertain | agree | strongly agree

16) I am coping well with my pain.

strongly disagree | disagree | uncertain | agree | strongly agree

17) My pain makes me feel useless and not needed.

strongly disagree | disagree | uncertain | agree | strongly agree

18) All my problems are caused by pain.

strongly disagree | disagree | uncertain | agree | strongly agree

19) I manage to do most things in my life that I want to do.

strongly disagree | disagree | uncertain | agree | strongly agree

Now see how you fared. Questions 1, 16 and 19 score: strongly disagree, 1; disagree, 2; uncertain, 3; agree, 4; strongly agree 5. All other questions score: strongly disagree, 5; disagree, 4; uncertain, 3; agree, 2; strongly agree, 1.

Most people with long-standing pain problems achieve somewhere around 50 on this test. If your score is above 65, then you are probably coping quite well with your pain and not allowing it to interfere with your life a great deal. The higher the score, the better you are at managing your life.

A score below 40 means that you are very likely having

difficulty living a normal life. You may feel a loss of confidence and have perhaps stopped mixing with people. Basically, you do not feel very happy with yourself and possibly feel that pain is controlling you. It is likely that you need some help in improving your coping skills.

The longer you have pain, the more likely the probability you will feel depressed. Even in normal circumstances people tend to brood over their problems when they feel under the weather. Pain magnifies black moods, making it harder to change your habits and behaviour.

You have probably gathered by now how difficult it is to quantify pain because what you are trying to measure is a personal experience which, quite often, you believe no one else fully understands. Even when the pain is all psychological, however, and there are no obvious physical symptoms, it is no less real.

It is common for people suffering long-term pain to become depressed and, conversely, for patients suffering depression to experience aches and pains they would not normally have. This is because there is a link between pain and depression which is important to understand.

Depression is not an isolated feeling but something that may take the form of a physical experience. Chemicals released in the brain during some forms of depression are also transmitters of pain messages, which is why 60 per cent of depression sufferers also experience pain of one kind or another.

A woman, for example, suffered a back pain whose origins could not be pinpointed until she began to talk about her life. It emerged that her husband had lost his job and they had no money to pay their rent. Their domestic situation had brought on depression which resulted in pain. Her case proved particularly easy to address. When Social Security benefits were arranged to ease their financial situation, the pain cleared up.

Broadly, there are two kinds of depression. *Reactive* depression is experienced when your house is uninsured and burns down, the family walk out and, on top of everything, the budgie dies. The most common cause of depression in people with chronic pain is a reaction to their pain and what is happening to them as they lose control of their lives. However, like the chicken and the egg, it is important to realise that, in some people, the problem starts off with depression, which causes the pain.

Endogenous depression, which means growing from within as opposed to reacting to outside circumstances, is the result of biochemical changes within the brain and is a medical condition. The sufferer may have a successful career, a loving family and a wonderful future, but still feels terribly, inexplicably depressed.

Like pain, it would be futile to say that this depression is imagined. Obviously, the person who is so miserable actually feels miserable and no doctor would suggest that he is not. In the same way, it is equally futile to say that someone who feels in pain is not feeling it, even if the cause might be psychological or because of depression.

Depression is one of the most common psychological difficulties that turn up the volume control of pain. The link between pain and depression makes chronic pain sufferers feel cut off from other people and unable to do things they used to do. They often lose their confidence and feel a sense of diminished control. As they become more and more isolated, their world becomes increasingly dominatedby pain and depression increases.

If you feel yourself coming down or sliding into a trough of depression, the most effective way to get through it is to activate yourself. Generally, when you try to head off a bout of depression, or lift yourself from it, anything you can do that gives you a sense of regaining control of your life is therapeutic. It may be a regular exercise or relaxation programme, or even something as small as doing a crossword or reading a book. The aim is to achieve an element of success and to experience the feeling of being in control again.

Chronic pain is an isolating experience and it is easy to feel quite cut off and alone. There is always benefit in mixing with other people as much as possible and keeping active, which is why relaxation groups, yoga classes and T'ai Chi sessions can be particularly helpful.

There are other manifestations of psychological pain which are more extreme and less commonly encountered. In some patients, for example, phobias may be expressed in terms of very real pain. In cases of delusion, patients often continue to suffer pain whatever treatments are administered.

Perfectionism, which is a kind of obsession, is another psychological dimension of pain. No matter how low this type of patient manages to turn down the pain volume he is never satisfied that it is enough. Only a complete absence of pain will meet the exacting demands he places on himself.

This is another example of unreasonable ideals which work against overcoming pain. If this type of person has a pain which is of quite a low level, say one out of ten, he is often unable to cope because his perfectionism stops him accepting any pain at all. Consequently, he will amplify his pain intensity several times over because he is deeply unhappy. A more easy-going individual would possibly not even notice a pain level so low.

There are also patients who, for many reasons, have excruciating pain for which no physical cause can be traced. The treatment is often unorthodox, but underlines the importance of understanding the psychological background to each individual problem.

Patients on the Pain Management Programme were talking about work one day, when a woman jokingly referred to her supervisor as a pain in the neck. Everyone laughed until someone remarked that the patient's problem was, in fact, a pain in the neck. She had been told by her doctor that she had arthritis in her spine, but an examination had indicated that there was not sufficient arthritis to justify this theory.

When she was questioned further about work, she recalled that her pain had briefly cleared up the week her supervisor had been on holiday. When the patient herself was on holiday the pain also improved, which led her to believe that rest had a beneficial effect. 'Work makes it worse,' she remarked, then realized for the first time that it was not her job, but her supervisor, with whom there was often friction, that caused her pain.

The patient changed her job and took up similar work in another factory. She still had a little pain, but was able to function quite happily. It was a case of a boss quite literally being a pain in the neck.

Another woman had suffered from a pain in her leg for five years for which her doctor and staff on the Pain Management Course could find no explanation. They knew that she was widowed but had no idea of the cause of her psychological pain until she spoke of her husband's death.

He had been hit by a car and taken to an Intensive Care Unit where doctors decided that his badly crushed leg would have to be amputated. His wife, who thought his leg was simply broken, was shocked when she was told that the leg had had to be removed. Shortly afterwards, her husband died.

As she talked more about the traumatic experience, she recalled that her pain had begun as she walked out of hospital after hearing about her husband's emergency operation. The pain was in the same leg that her husband had had amputated.

It was felt that this was the reason why she was in chronic pain, but she refused to accept it and continued to insist that the cause was physical and no doctor had been able to diagnose it.

The woman left the programme and was last heard of still seeking a cure. The staff had found to their satisfaction what had caused the pain but, sadly, the conclusion was not to the patient's satisfaction.

Another patient attended the programme with a burning facial pain. Nothing physically wrong could be found, though there was no doubt that she was genuinely suffering. It was eventually traced back to when she was 16 and intervened in a fight between her father and mother. The father struck a blow at the mother which landed on the girl's face.

She ran from the house in shock to her boyfriend's, where his family took her in. The patient was too frightened to go back to her parents and married her boyfriend. Soon afterwards, her mother and father divorced and then died. Her pain was associated with guilt because she had left her mother and because she had never made it up with her father before his death. After a course of psychoanalysis her facial pain disappeared.

These are unusual cases, but they illustrate how deep-rooted psychological pain can become and how important it is to increase your understanding of yourself and develop an awareness of your thoughts, feelings and actions.

When chronic pain takes hold of people's thoughts and emotions, it begins to dictate the way they behave in everyday life. Chronic pain sufferers send out signals that they have a problem. It may be through facial expressions, rubbing their back, limping, wearing a surgical collar or perhaps spending most of their time in a wheelchair.

It is important to ask yourself what kind of signals your pain is sending out. A psychological situation many long-term pain sufferers find themselves locked into is that pain makes them 'special'. People ask how they are feeling, help out with the shopping or strenuous work and solicitously inquire if they have had their tablets.

Life appears to offer a number of bonuses when they cast themselves in the role of pain victim. When they were well, they probably received only a fraction of the attention and worked hard for their family with little acknowledgement or appreciation.

Domestic pets discover that, if they behave in a certain way, they get a reward and some pain sufferers have unconsciously learned similar behaviour. If they send out signals of pain and suffering, people around them react in a favourable manner.

Once you condition yourself to avoid doing things because of pain, your behaviour becomes a difficult habit to break. It is like someone limping to avoid pain and continuing when the injury has healed because it brought them help and attention.

Behaving in a certain way to side-step something unpleasant is similar to the little boy who banged a bass drum around the streets all day to keep the lions and tigers away.

'But there aren't any lions and tigers,' someone said.

'See how well it works,' he replied.

Once avoidance behaviour begins it is difficult to stop. It helps to keep the cycle of pain revolving until, in some cases, patients actually prefer being pain victims because, despite the suffering, it gives their life a dimension it previously lacked.

An effective method of helping yourself to break pain habits is by gradually reducing negative actions through targeting – setting small, achievable objectives which unlearn bad pain behaviour and promote positive activity. If you sit in a wheelchair to avoid pain, or wear a collar for the same reason, you can work on a programme which will gradually reduce the time you spend doing this each day.

Some people feel that pain may not have affected their life to any great degree. If this is genuinely the case, then it is still a good idea to think about areas of your life in which you would like to see change. It can be difficult to become motivated and we all find at times that it is easy to get into a rut and put off things which need to be done. The purpose of targeting is to consider ways of reversing the changes pain has made in your life. In order to set a target you need to take time to honestly assess what these changes are. Here are a few examples of activities which may have been curtailed by pain:

- Social life – refusing invitations to visit friends, go to parties, the local pub or on family outings.
- Travelling in cars, buses and trains.
- Driving.
- Housework – certain chores may be difficult because of bending, etc.
- Gardening.
- Shopping.
- Sitting for long periods of time – this may, for example, affect going to the cinema or theatre.
- Walking distances.

Having identified an area you would like to change, you need to draw up guidelines to help you set your target. It may be that you want to pursue a particular target that will require some time to achieve. Do not let this put you off. It may be possible to take a gradual approach, increasing your activity step by step until, eventually, you have successfully achieved it.

Guidelines for Targeting

1 Consider an area you really want to change or improve upon.

2 Be realistic about your target. Try not to choose a task that

is initially too far beyond your capabilities. Alternatively, do not succumb to bad pain behaviour and under-estimate yourself.

3 Be specific so that you can measure your achievements.

4 Try not to incorporate too many variables: make sure your selection is not too dependent on other people, good weather, etc. In other words, when you make a contract with yourself, do not build in an escape clause.

5 Always be positive.

6 Consider the possibility, if you wish, of setting yourself more than one target.

Targeting is a useful way of understanding more about yourself. Pain has a habit of blurring the edges of reality, so it is important to use techniques to rediscover yourself and examine why and how you may have changed with pain.

When pain is the most important thing in your life, a meeting with your doctor can crucially affect which direction your emotions take. How you react to your doctor's comments and observations can generate feelings which, in some cases, may actually lead to your pain increasing. Many feel that their doctors have been rude, off-hand, kept them waiting for long periods and dismissed their pain as imaginary.

Many patients react to the way they feel they have been treated with anger and a sense of isolation, rejection and depression. Some say: 'I go to my GP or consultant expecting success. When I don't find it, I feel lost and let down. I don't know where to turn.' They tend to be people who hoped that their doctor would take control and lift their pain from them. When she or he was unable to do so, they felt abandoned and in limbo. 'I didn't know what to do,' one patient recalled. 'I felt I couldn't go on after that.'

It was only when they discovered the Pain Management Programme that they learned that the solution lay with them. In effect, after visiting many doctors, they had become the real specialist in their own pain. No one else could experience it or know what it was like because it belonged only to them. Harbouring resentment and anger towards their doctor only resulted in prolonging their pain.

Another common complaint is that visiting different doctors often achieves little more than being offered different explanations. One doctor would give one reason for their pain, while another might suggest something else entirely. These patients never felt they were getting the same answer twice and were left in a state of increasing confusion.

It is possible that the doctors, perhaps sensing that they desperately wanted an explanation, felt obliged to offer them one. It was only when they reached a pain clinic, and met a doctor who specialized in pain, that they encountered someone with the courage to say: 'I don't know why you've got this pain. I can only guess at it. How to go on from here is now the real issue.'

In some cases, patients cannot understand their pain because no one can. They are searching for an explanation that is somehow structured and easy to understand; something they can visualize and grasp. Having received it, the next question is: 'So, why can't you make me better?'

People too obsessed with the mechanism of their pain – striving to discover exactly what the reasons are for it – struggle to apply logic to something which may be impossible to achieve. Trying to offload their problem onto a doctor and then blaming him when he cannot provide a miracle is not taking full responsibility for their pain. Unless they accept responsibility, they cannot hope to regain control.

Their GP, of course, is not a specialist and it would be unreasonable to expect him to have a detailed knowledge of the fifty or so specialized branches of medicine. However, it is equally fair to say that the way he deals with long-term pain patients can greatly influence their psychological approach to their problems.

Some GPs may try one treatment and then another, searching for ways to help and, when they have finally exhausted their options, inform their patient out of the blue that there is nothing they can do to help. The result is that the patient believes his situation is hopeless and feelings of anger and isolation understandably build up.

Other doctors took the view that they had a deal, a contract, with their patient and when they took on their case, said: 'We will try a, b and c and, if they don't work, that's really all we are able to do, but we'll give it our best shot.' Their patients reported that they did not feel as abandoned because their doctor had been honest and fulfilled his part of the bargain.

Honesty is a great asset. Many pain sufferers run such a gauntlet of symptoms, thoughts and emotions between consultations that it is difficult to keep track of how they feel and what they expect from their doctor. If you experience such problems it is better to put time aside and work out simply what questions you would like your doctor to answer. Write them down and, on your next visit, explain that it is difficult in the short time available to say clearly what is on your mind and refer to your sheet of paper.

Problems and resentment arise when a patient, who may have a life of pain, feels that he is only being allocated two minutes to what is the most important thing in the world to him.

Assembling your thoughts and speaking your mind clearly without the distraction of negative feelings often requires a little assertiveness. Businessmen frequently use assertiveness in their training. It does not mean aggression, but a tactful, honest and straightforward way of informing people about what you want. Assertiveness is a useful asset for regaining control over your life. It may mean choosing not to speak out or, on occasions, choosing to lose an argument. It may mean admitting mistakes, being gentle and tactful and allowing other people to be assertive, too.

Thinking carefully about what you say and expressing yourself honestly and diplomatically cannot offend people. If it does, then that is their problem, not yours. Making efforts to be more assertive will develop your confidence, help you to take control of your emotions and to regain control of your own situation.

Trying to understand more about yourself and studying how your thoughts, feeling and actions relate to pain will help you cope more effectively.

REMEMBER

- Try not to let pain dominate what you do or what you think about. Try not to dwell on pain or think about it too much. It helps if you can distract yourself by keeping busy and interested in as many other things as possible.

- Try not to avoid doing things because of your pain. Don't use your pain as an excuse not to do something - not even to yourself. Try to keep control of what you do and not allow pain to dominate your life too much.

- Try not to talk about your pain. Try to look as fit and healthy as possible. Never make a show of being in pain, either by talking about it or by actions which may signal others that you have a pain problem.

- Try not to be too negative. try to always think about positive aspects of your life and concentrate on good things that are happening.

- Don't look for a miracle cure. They very rarely happen and, while you are waiting, things usually get much worse.

- Take control of yourself. Learn relaxation techniques, take regular exercise and keep yourself as mentally and physically active as you can. Keep up your interests and relationships with other people. When you increase what you are doing, increase your activities gradually. Don't try to do too much too soon.

7

Pain and other people

The poet John Donne pondered the idea that no man is an island, a thought particularly apposite for people in chronic pain. Everyone thrives on attention – without it we would suffer from emotional starvation. Pain sufferers generally send out more signals for attention than family, friends and workmates who do not have the same health problems. Because your pain demands attention from you, in turn your behaviour demands attention from others. It may be a pained expression, a gesture indicating suffering, a groan, a tone of voice, a wince or a dozen other ways in which you transmit to the world that all is not well.

Pain is the cuckoo in the nest of normal living. As it occupies your time, it grows bigger, demanding more and more until feelings of happiness, confidence and self-esteem are elbowed out. Your subconscious, like an anxious mother bird, constantly reminds you that the monster which has taken over requires increasing time and attention.

Pain has a voracious appetite for attention. No matter how much time you devote to pain, it usually demands more. Without realising it, you may be constantly sending out signals for sympathy and attention. It is similar to screech behaviour in babies touched on in an earlier chapter. The baby learns that if it screams it will be picked up. When the harrassed mother tries not to pick it up, it screams louder. In the same way, pain sufferers may subconsciously turn up the volume control of their pain to gain attention from family and friends. Unfortunately, in the process, they increase and prolong their own suffering.

If, for example, you complain of a headache, your partner may be very understanding and offer to do the dishes. If you complain again after dinner the following evening, they may be a little less sympathetic. After a week of this behaviour, you would almost certainly not be guaranteed their original response. To obtain the attention you received on day one, you would by now probably have to writhe on the floor clutching your head.

To achieve the level of attention your pain demands, you have to increase your suffering. Your subconscious, desperately needing a reaction of sympathy, tenderness, concern, support or help, turns up the pain volume by opening the gates to obtain the response it previously acquired with only a small amount of pain.

If you are in chronic pain, it is important to ask yourself if your family and friends only tend to take notice when you cast yourself in the role of a pain victim.

When you send out pain signals, there are usually two ways in which those around you react – both of them wrong. They are either unsympathetic and ignore you, starving you of attention and refusing to believe you are in pain; or, possibly worse, they become over-attentive, doing jobs for you and offering help at every opportunity. They force you to adopt the role of an invalid.

When this kind of suffocating behaviour is prolonged it can sometimes turn relatives into dynamic seekers after a cure. They wheel their partner from doctor to doctor and speak completely on his or her behalf. The patient becomes a glove puppet, almost an inanimate object, while the husband or wife, who does not have the pain, takes over the show.

Pain sufferers are not the only recipients of such behaviour. People with any type of chronic illness tend to be dismissed. Radio 4's programme for the disabled, *Does He Take Sugar?*, borrowed its title from a furious wheelchair patient who was addressed through his wife as though he did not exist.

This kind of reaction is demeaning to pain sufferers, removing their dignity, confidence and self-respect. It is easy to be judgemental about relatives who act this way, but there is every possibility that the patient has encouraged much of it by sending out helpless signals. Families of pain sufferers have to walk a fine line. There is a delicate balance between ignoring someone in chronic pain and trying to do too much for them. Starving someone of attention is as unkind as suffocating them with it.

If you treat someone as ill, then they become ill. The point was illustrated by some mischievous medical students who decided to play a joke on a particularly obnoxious colleague. When he came into the common room, they remarked that he looked quite pale and asked if he felt all right. The student protested that he had never felt better. Then, more students walked in and made similar comments. This went on until, by the end of the afternoon, he convinced himself that he was ill and, amid great hilarity, slipped out to the Casualty Department for a check-up.

The same principle worked for African witch doctors who could kill people because everyone believed they had the power to do it. If the witch doctor told someone that they were going to die then, generally, they would. This does not work in our society because we are not conditioned to believe it. However, it is possible to make someone ill simply by the way you treat them.

If a member of your family is in chronic pain, there are three useful guidelines:

- Encourage your relative to be as active as possible. Don't talk about or dwell on the pain too much. Try not to overdo the sympathy. Don't keep asking, for example, 'How's the pain today?' or 'How are you feeling?' This only reminds your relative that he has pain and will probably make things worse.
- Encourage your relative to be as independent as possible. Try not to do too much for them.
- If your relative dwells on pain, or talks about it constantly, try to change the subject or distract them with something more interesting. Encourage them to take exercise, to learn relaxation skills, take up interests and to think about more positive aspects of their life.

Staff on the Pain Management Programme are trained to handle attention-seeking displays of pain behaviour. The fact that someone is broadcasting their pain really means that their subconscious is trying to attract attention or divert them from exercise, relaxation, or whatever efforts they are making to overcome pain. The more determined they are to take positive steps and conquer their disability, the louder their subconscious screams that they are a pain patient and deserve some attention.

It may be verbal, in the form of groans, sighs, 'ouches' and complaints; visual, by limping, restless movements, tortured facial expressions or rubbing the painful area; it may be expressed in agitated, tense, depressed or withdrawn behaviour; or in using equipment, such as collars, corsets, slings, sticks, crutches, wheelchairs and gadgets.

Groaning, limping or withdrawing into yourself does not help the pain, but is simply a form of communication to tell people you are in distress. It may be considered unkind to make similar comments about surgical appliances, but there is no scientific evidence to suggest that many of these devices are more than a psychological prop. To wear them for a few weeks is fine, but people who have been walking around for two years in a corset or collar display them as a badge to announce that they are disabled. It is almost medically impossible to support the neck or spine by means of a collar or corset. They tend to make the muscles stiff and tense and, when the appliance is removed after prolonged use, the muscles are by then too weak to support the affected area. The patient has to put the collar back on to help to do the work the muscles have become unable to perform.

Sufferers who make pain faces, or clutch at themselves, are not helping their pain, and this is really just a signal that their pain is fighting to retain its hold on their subconscious. People who persist in being positive can pass through this barrier and firmly establish who is in charge. It is important to recognise that your pain, and the way it makes you feel and act, has a significant effect on others. If you send out messages that you are in pain, people will treat you as an invalid, not an individual. The way they treat you will, in turn, determine how well you cope. Whether you complain that you hurt and can't do anything, or simply send out non-verbal messages, amounts to the same. People respond to what you broadcast.

Chronic pain patients often deny that they send out such obvious pain messages, but conversations with their partners disprove the view. One interview, typical of many, ran:

> Doctor: 'Do you know when he is in pain?'
> Patient's Wife: 'Yes, I can always tell.'
> Doctor: 'And what do you do then?'
> Patient's Wife: 'I'm sympathetic. I tell him to sit down and I rub his back. I offer to do the dishes, or whatever he can't manage.'

One patient, David, sustained multiple fractures when a car hit him, throwing him 20 feet. He joined the Pain Management Programme in its first week, heavily stooped and walking with a stick. He had remained at work but found office life difficult to cope with. His biggest complaint was:

> 'If only people would treat me normally. They regard me as a cripple. I never get asked to do ordinary things any more, such as making the tea. It's very demeaning.'

When David was asked how people knew he was disabled, he supposed that it was because he used a stock and kept it handy on his desk. It was suggested that, if he could manage without it, it might be better to leave it in his car.

He tried this and wrote several weeks later:

> 'I feel great. Yesterday, someone in the office said: 'Come on, David, it's your turn to make the tea. Don't think you can get out of it.' They accepted me as normal. And,

because they made me feel normal, it is now much easier to cope.'

It is important to become aware of pain signals, make every effort to reduce them to a minimum and persuade your family and friends to treat you normally. Patients on the Pain Management Programme are encouraged to look as fit and healthy as they possibly can. Rather than discuss what they are unable to do, or how much pain they have, they are urged to talk about what they can do and the targets they have achieved. It is more positive to talk about the five minutes someone has spent walking than the twelve hours they have spent lying in bed.

Success depends on families working together, but this is not always easy. One patient, Doris, suffered from a bad back after an operation and had difficulty standing or lifting. She was the centre of her family and worked hard looking after her husband and three grown-up sons. Her ambition was to return home and cook the Sunday lunch.

Doris set herself targets, breaking them down to work on all the aspects of cooking a meal: standing for an hour, lifting weights comparable to a full saucepan, bending to put things into the oven. The meal was a great success but the event turned into a disaster. When her family finished Sunday lunch, they disappeared to the pub, leaving Doris with the washing up, which she found difficult to cope with. They assumed that, because she had cooked a meal, she was better.

They should have invited her to join them or, if she found the walk too difficult, offered to stay at home to keep her company. Instead, they ignored her. Doris had to explain that they needed to be more supportive and that her big day had turned out to be a disappointment.

Chronic pain inevitably affects your relationships with family, friends and workmates. The wrong kind of pain behaviour occurs when pain has eroded your confidence and sense of self-worth. The position pain forces you into and the resulting demands you place on people around you diminish your self-esteem and desire to succeed.

Actions and feelings relating to pain are closely linked. It is difficult, for example, to slump in a chair with your shoulders hunched and say aloud: 'I feel great'. Somehow, it lacks conviction. Equally, it feels odd to throw back your shoulders, stick out your chest, punch the air and shout: 'I feel depressed'. How you act sends signals inwardly to yourself as well as outwardly to others.

Self-esteem is feeling good about yourself, knowing that people like you and acquiring confidence and control over your emotions.

American business research indicates that two out of three people don't enjoy what they do. It is not unusual for people in positions of power and authority to feel pressured, depressed and constantly under criticism. At the Pain Management Programme training tapes for business executives and athletes are adapted to the problems of chronic pain. Pain patients have an even greater need to think positively and succeed.

Body language – awareness of what signals your body is sending out – has a profound effect on both yourself and others. Even sitting in the right position affects your mind and how you feel about yourself. When you feel down and sink into yourself there is no room for your diaphragm to move and you take the kind of small, shallow breaths associated with depression. Sitting straight, getting yourself and your spirits as high as possible, improves the way you feel.

There are times when even high-flying professionals feel anxiety and a loss of control in stressful situations. This is a familiar situation to many chronic pain sufferers. Professional public speakers use a way of calming themselves and regaining control, called the Sarnoff Squeeze.

The method is to squeeze the palms of your hands together while breathing in. The deeper you inhale, the more tightly you squeeze together your hands. When your lungs are full, exhale slowly while releasing the pressure on your palms. Anxiety ebbs away, replaced by a feeling of calmness and control. If the exercise is too conspicuous to do when other people are around, you can achieve the same results by pressing your palms against the arms of a chair.

People with chronic pain are often unhappy with their bodies. As pain progresses, making life miserable, they sometimes develop resentment against the particular part that gives them problems. This is not unusual, as most of us have some aspect of our bodies we wish could be more perfect. Pain merely exaggerates these feelings in a negative way.

Feeling comfortable about your body is part of learning to like yourself and rebuilding self-esteem. It is unreasonable to expect people to like you and afford you respect if you do not look upon yourself the same way. Some people tend to live their lives as Robin Reliants wishing they were Rolls Royces. When they are unhappy with themselves, they tend to lock themselves in a mental garage, turn off their engine and say: 'I'm not going anywhere. I'm going to sit here and wait until I become a Rolls.'

Pain makes people react this way, retreating into themselves in the hope that, one day, everything will be all right. Like the car, they will probably succeed only in becoming more and more rusty until they are unable to move.

A good example is post-herpetic neuralgia, a pain which goes on intolerably after nerve damage from shingles, especially in elderly people. Many sufferers do as little as possible, thinking, 'When the pain goes, I'll restart my life.' They wait and, after a year, find they have the same amount of pain. They stop visiting their friends, going to the shops, doing the housework or seeing their family.

After perhaps three or four years of this, they consult their doctor who probably prescribes pain killers. They should realise instead that, while their pain may be around for another four years, the quality of their lives is slipping away. The only advice of any practical value is not to wait but to become active again.

Pain patients who lose confidence because of their bodies find it difficult to maintain relationships with other people. A useful exercise, which may help, is aimed at making friends with your body again, becoming more aware of it and accepting pain without resentment.

It works like this: Take off your clothes, standing in front of a full-length mirror and take stock of yourself. Starting at the top of your head with your hair, move down your body, making a list of all the parts you dislike or which you consider are less than perfect. You may wish for your hair to be curly instead of straight, that your ears are slightly too big, your nose is too small, and so on. Be as objective as possible, as though the body you are looking at belongs to someone else. As you travel down, concentrate, too, on the parts you are happy with, feeling pleased that you are comfortable with them.

When you have studied yourself, right down to your toes, go back to the beginning and place a hand on the first part of your body that you felt unhappy with. Say aloud: 'I'm sorry for criticising you and disliking you. You've been a good (arm, leg, stomach etc). You've done your best over the years. You're not perfect, but you're part of me. I haven't been able to function properly because of you, but I love you.'

At first, you may feel self-conscious doing this exercise, but it is a private dialogue between you and your body. It concerns no one else and is an effective way of being more kind to yourself. Many people come to terms with themselves and feel more at ease after doing this exercise.

If you are in pain you need to feel good about yourself and

the environment you find yourself in, even if it may not be positive or supportive. No one can guarantee that wherever they go, whether to the local shop or an interview for a job, that people are going to be kind and understanding. Self-confidence and self-esteem are built by feeling good about yourself even when people may not be feeling good towards you. The aim is not to become reliant on others for the way you feel about yourself. If you are in chronic pain, what you transmit is possibly negative and what you send out governs the messages you are going to receive back and how they affect you.

When you are in pain your subconscious constantly urges you to play safe. This, as we know, is not wise advice. When you look back on your life, all the major decisions you have made have been based on risk. Taking exams, your first date, getting married all carried a risk of failure, but an overriding hope that they would work out. Changing your life always involves risk, but change is difficult if you lack confidence. Life, in this respect, is a little like playing poker. You may not have a good hand but, if you appear confident, you increase your chances of winning. Confidence and self-esteem go hand in hand to improve your image of yourself and your relationships with others. They enable you to attend a job interview, or be in a situation which perhaps does not work out, and carry on playing.

The first step in building these positive aspects to help you overcome pain is to make an all-out effort to eliminate negative pain behaviour.

One important question to ask yourself: Do you ever use your pain as an excuse to get out of doing something? If you do, there may be other issues to sort out in your life before you can go forward and take on your main objective of conquering pain.

Pain is like a balance sheet. On one side, there occasionally appear to be benefits – pain gets you attention, it helps you avoid doing things you don't enjoy, at times there are even financial compensations. But there is a debit side. Once you try to use pain to your advantage, it always comes back to trap you in a worse situation.

A good example of this is accident compensation. If, say, you are run over by a bus, the accident may leave you a nervous wreck, suffering pain, depression and lack of confidence. This is a real condition which a court would probably recognize entitles you to a settlement. On the face of it, this seems a just and reasonable financial compensation for injuries you have suffered. It is also a situation in which pain makes your conscious and subconscious pull in opposite directions.

While, consciously, you might reason: 'I'd give anything if this pain would go away and I could return to a normal life', your subconscious, which is always more simplistic, reasons differently. It argues: 'The bus hit him. It wasn't his fault. He's entitled to redress. The more he hurts, the more he stands to receive. So let's tighten the muscles, wind up the pain volume and see some justice.'

This may be the way you feel about the accident, but what your subconscious fails to appreciate is the simple fact that when you hurt, your life is miserable. The part of you arguing for justice and turning up the pain to get more compensation is not in touch with the conscious part which would do anything to feel well again. The result is that you may receive the money which is rightly yours, but you end up in much more pain than you need to be.

Doctors, psychologists and courts understand the money you receive will never make you better. Compensation is paid in order to try and minimize the influence of the accident on your life. This financial benefit of pain almost always backfires, however – in the long term it does little to help you. In the long term, however, it does little to help you.

Sometimes, it helps to be more honest with yourself and ask what lies behind your reasons for acting and thinking a certain way. Neville Shone, a patient on the Pain Management Programme, made this voyage of self-discovery and went on to write a book about his experiences, which we highly recommend. He had had a benign tumour removed from his spine and, although the operation was successful, his spinal cord was partially damaged, leaving him with chronic back pain.

When Neville's wife asked him to help her with the Saturday shopping, he complained that his back was hurting and used the pain as an excuse to get out of something he did not enjoy. Instead, he spent the afternoon pleasantly watching TV. Then, Neville realized that he had to accept that his pain also prevented him from driving into town to visit his friends and from attending a football match in the afternoon. By turning up his pain volume to avoid shopping, he had also missed the activities he really enjoyed.

On the Pain Management Programme, Neville thought about his actions more carefully and decided to take another approach. What he should have said, he realized, was something like: 'I've got back pain and I don't particularly enjoy shopping. I don't want to make it worse doing something I don't find much fun. If you can manage the shopping, I'll have a rest and we could go to the cinema tonight. It may make my back hurt, but at least we will have a good time together.'

By accepting that he was going to have pain regardless, he opted for having pain doing something he would enjoy. His wife had no objection to shopping alone and looked forward to an evening with her husband. The decision also left him free to see his friends.

Sexual relationships are an area where pain is often used as an avoidance excuse, by men as often as women. 'Not tonight, dear, I've a headache', is a cliche which has become part of English comedy folklore. The partner who makes the excuse may not have a massive headache, but uses it to get out of sex for another reason. Instead of saying, perhaps, 'I don't want sex because your feet smell', the partner is saying, 'I don't want sex because there is something wrong with me.'

This is another illusionary 'benefit' of pain – by telling a white lie, one partner avoids sex without hurting the other's feelings. Unfortunately, in the long term, it does not resolve the problems of their relatonship. If, to put it lightly, smelly feet are the only thing stopping you having sex, you should persuade your partner to wash his feet.

Further problems arise when someone experiences a genuine headache to avoid sex because they don't want to face up to the issues involved.

Men, in particular, can develop backache to rationalize subconscious fears of impotence or a belief that they cannot perform well sexually. Rather than be honest with their partner, they suffer real backache. Pain excuses always come back to trap you in a worse situation. Whether the excuse was originally made consciously or subconsciously is immaterial. After a period of behaving this way, it becomes no longer a white lie but real pain. You may have avoided sex, but you are now also missing work, going out with friends and many other things you want to do.

S.P.O.D. – the Association to Aid the Sexual and Personal Relationships of People with a Disability – is an organization which helps the disabled to enjoy a healthy love life. One of its golden rules is that love, patience and mutual tolerance on the part of both partners seldom fails to solve problems and most difficulties can be overcome. As the work of SPOD successfully demonstrates, it is almost impossible not to have sex if you really want to. Unlike many of SPOD's clients, chronic pain sufferers have more possibility of improving their condition and leading a normal sexual life.

If you have back pain, for example, it is not an excuse for

avoiding having sex. If you say or believe otherwise, then you should look beyond this for other reasons: Do you no longer enjoy sex? Do you have marital relationship problems? Do you have fears of no longer performing adequately? If these issues are not addressed, then there is less possibility of overcoming your pain. Many psychologists would say that, if these other problems are put right, then the pain might no longer have reason for continuing and could perhaps lessen or disappear completely.

It remains a fact that sexual activity can be uncomfortable for chronic pain sufferers, but most people go on because they consider it important. The discomfort it causes is worth it. Pain isolates people and prises relationships apart, in some cases destroying them. Sex not only helps to keep a loving relationship intact, but tells your subconscious that you are not giving in to pain's demands.

Most pain problems, whether sexual or concerning day-to-day living, have a solution if you search hard enough. Arnold, an elderly patient attending the Pain Management Programme, lived for crown green bowling. The worst thing about his pain was that it stopped him taking part in local matches. When team mates rang to ask why he had not turned up, he told them that his back made travelling too painful. Staying at home and curtailing his social life upset him, until he thought about it more deeply and realized that he was not being entirely honest. The truth was that he had become forgetful with age and the bus company had changed its routes to the bowling green. He now had to take two buses instead of one and found it confusing. Often, he arrived late for a match or spent hours getting home again.

Arnold obviously could not tell his friends that he felt confused and worried about becoming senile, so he used his back pain as an excuse instead. When he discussed this someone suggested that he should persuade one of his friends to give him a lift to the green. He took up the idea and continued to lead an active life. His back pain was not bad enough to prevent him playing bowls – it was the other problems that had prevented him from enjoying himself. The lesson of Arnold's tale, like many others, is that when you use pain as an excuse to avoid social relationships, it always comes back to trap you.

Once this problem is resolved, there are many ways to improve your confidence and self-esteem and move towards normal life again.

Your subconscious always plays safe, believing that hurt is harm. At the slightest twinge, it reminds you that you are a pain patient and life is miserable. It constantly nags you to not do too much, that it is unwise to go out, exercise or lead a normal life. This does not have to be a one-way conversation. When you are in pain, much of your life is spent tuning into your subconscious, drifting away into useless thoughts and wishing you were well again. You listen passively, as though taking in a radio play. Things often begin to change, however, when you realize that you can talk back. You can broadcast to your subconscious and have just as much influence over it as it has been exerting over you for all these years.

Because your subconscious is not terribly bright and sees things only in a very simple way which it believes are in your best interests, repetition may reinforce the message that you are going to live your own life. You are no longer in the passenger seat, but behind the wheel. Changing your lifestyle, as we have seen, is the only effective way to convince your subconscious that you mean business. Repeating positive statements to yourself underlines the message.

One effective way to build your self-esteem is by saying aloud quietly that you are loveable and capable. By doing this on waking, sometime during the day, and last thing at night, you are sending a message to your subconscious that you are a nice person and that you can accomplish things.

It is important not simply to say the words, but to think positively about what you mean. As you repeat the phrase, think about someone who loves you, what their affection means and about how capable you are. There are many things we may do well – driving, cooking, handwriting – that give a sense of achievement. After about two months, less in many cases, what you are saying submerges itself into your subconscious and becomes part of your life.

The technique is not as unusual as it may appear. We all hold conversations with ourselves every day, but rarely in a positive way.

More commonly, we say things like: 'I can't be bothered', 'I'm sick and tired of this', or 'I can't see myself doing that', which are all negative feelings signalling to your subconscious that you haven't the energy, or determination, to do something.

You are only likely to do things if you can see yourself doing them. For example, you may long to give up smoking but, if you cannot honestly see yourself in a year's time walking around without cigarettes in your pocket, then there is little chance of succeeding.

When you visualize yourself doing something, it is naturally much easier to accomplish when the time comes. In America, top basketball players are encouraged to visualize the ball dropping into the net to improve their performance. Research has shown that sportsmen who play sport in their minds become better sportsmen more quickly than those who do not use that ability.

When you are in pain, negative thoughts are not easy to stop. Instead of tuning in to them and becoming more downcast and anxious, you should cut them off by saying a command to yourself. It may be 'cancel' or 'stop' – anything appropriate will do – and the effect can be surprising.

The problem with negative thoughts is that if you are, say, angry, they can go round and round in your head for hours. It becomes difficult to think about anything, apart from how angry you feel, or how unfair life has been. You may feel guilty about something you have said and then feel angry for feeling guilty and so on. Unless you firmly stop it, you can spend a whole day like this.

Negative thoughts are a waste of time and energy because they are not actually going anywhere. It is much easier to tell yourself: 'Stop. I'll perhaps think about that tomorrow.'

Both negative and positive thoughts are very powerful and have great bearing on the way we perceive ourselves. A therapist asked patients to describe themselves in terms of a tree, which allows scope for imagination and can be quite revealing. One patient with spine problems described an old oak, hollow and rotten in the middle and barely able to stand. This is the way he felt negatively affected by his pain and, as a result, the way in which he saw himself.

The therapist asked the patients to visualize an acorn dropping from this tree and the way it would grow. She talked of straight, firm shoots, healthy foliage and branches reaching skyward as the tree became taller and stronger. As she spoke, patients taking part in the exercise visibly straightened and sat more upright as they visualized it. The power of positive thought can have a marked effect on both our actions and feelings. This visual imagery was used here by our healer, but it can also be employed by psychologists, showing the link between some alternative techniques and the most progressive modern medicine.

People with chronic pain often dwell unnecessarily on remarks other people make. This is partly because pain erodes their confidence and makes them feel vulnerable. Often, the remark is unintentional but, occasionally, it can be quite deliberate and very cutting. If you work to re-build your self-esteem it is important to realize that no matter what anyone says or does to you, you are still a worthwhile person. Once you convince yourself – and your subconscious – that you are loveable and capable, the hurt of chance remarks diminishes. Your own belief in yourself deflects them like a shield.

It is in your interest to convey to people how well you feel, rather than how much pain you are suffering. Friends, family and workmates are unsure how to treat you when you complain of pain.

If, for example, someone asks how you are and you reply, 'Terrible', the scene for the conversation is immediately set. They feel wary and a little nervous because you are not feeling good. Someone who replies, 'Great', or 'Wonderful', puts the other person at ease. The conversation, from this point, is more likely to go up than down. It is surprising that saying, 'Great', even when you don't feel it, not only helps the other person, but actually lifts the conversation so that, by the end, you actually feel good yourself.

There are times, of course, when it is important to confide in someone how you feel, but only in the right situation. It is much better to develop a habit of being positive than gain a reputation for moaning. If pain has made you think and behave a certain way, it is equally possible to change things around by thinking and acting differently.

When you set yourself targets to change your life, it is natural that you may worry about succeeding. After all, you are attempting things which pain may have prevented you from doing for years. Once this happens there is a tendency for your mind to dredge up all your past failures and parade them one by one until you feel genuinely afraid of going on, or pushing yourself further.

One way to overcome this is to turn the emotion to your advantage. As far as your body is concerned, in terms of responses and chemical changes, there is very little difference between fear and excitement. It is only a small step from feeling afraid of new challenges to facing them with excitement and anticipation.

Success or failure may depend on exactly what type of thoughts you allow your mind to assemble. Looking back on a Wimbledon defeat, the great tennis player Navratilova reflected that if she had remembered all her past successes instead of worrying about failing, she would have won the match.

Past successes are an important part of sports psychology and business management. People display their trophies to remind them how successful they are. If you achieve a target of going out for the day, buy yourself something to keep to remind yourself of what you achieved. Some people open a bottle of wine to celebrate a success and write on the cork what the occasion was. A drawer full of corks or a mantelpiece of mementoes can be as much a morale-booster as a case full of silver trophies.

Of course people fail, too. But every failure is an experience which generates success. If you cycle round a corner too slowly, you will probably fall off but, next time, you will remember and do it perfectly. People who never take a risk because they are frightened of failing might as well remain in bed.

The more risks you take, the more likelihood there is that your life will change, your pain diminish and your relationships with others be restored to a happier, more fulfilled level.

help, or feel frustrated if they think their doctor does not believe them. It is easy to become obsessed about problems of this kind.

On the other side of the desk, from the doctor's point of view, it can be equally frustrating and distressing to have someone describe symptoms that you are unable to help. Sometimes, the chronic pain sufferer seems to make appointments week after week, demanding treatment which is simply not available.

Getting along with your doctor and getting the best from him is a two-way process. When you see your GP he obviously does not have a great deal of time to spend with each patient. It is best to think out what you are going to say in order to use the time wisely, to your greatest advantage.

Decide on the most important points you wish to get across. Primarily, your doctor needs a brief history of your symptoms and some idea of your main worries. Don't be unfair by bringing up a significant problem right at the end of the appointment, when he is running late. If you feel you need to write some points down for him to read, fine, but remember, he is your doctor, not your biographer!

Patients differ enormously. From a doctor's viewpoint, we see some people who offer little information and resent being asked about their problems, whilst others volunteer so much that there is no time to talk about their problems at the end of the consultation. The onus is not entirely on you – a good doctor will be able to direct the interview, asking questions which obtain the maximum amount of information from you.

If you have had your condition for some time and are worried about it, you may feel you require a second opinion. Your doctor may already have suggested this, anyway, and arranged for a specialist to see you. If not, it is quite reasonable for you to ask for a second opinion if you think it would be relevant.

The doctor only has to refer you for a second opinion if he feels it is medically indicated. He certainly does not have to go on referring you to specialists, if none of them seem able to help. There is a law of diminishing returns, and the more doctors you see, the less likely each one is to be able to do anything for you.

To help you get the maximum benefit from your appointment, if you have chronic pain, it is useful to have an idea of what the doctor is likely to need to know from you. Questions are likely to cover such areas as:

- When did the pain start?
- Why did it start?
- Did it come on gradually, or was it the result of an accident, a burst of unaccustomed activity, or some other sudden onset?
- What did you think about it when it first came on, and what did you do about it?
- Was it bad enough to seek medical advice, or did you wait to see if it got better by itself?

When you have answered his questions, he will want a brief history of the pain, together with the most significant factors which have influenced it. Even though the pain is important to you, it is not necessary to go into great detail. A succinct comment, such as: 'I had some physiotherapy, but it wasn't helpful for more than a few days,' is more useful than a blow-by-blow account of everything the physiotherapist did.

No matter how casual the consultation may appear, the doctor has an agenda through which he works to obtain as much information as possible. He will want to know, for example, how the pain has changed, if at all, over the days, months or years it has been present. Has it spread or diminished in the area it affects? Has it changed its nature, or its severity?

He will, of course, also want a description of the type of pain it is. Some people find this difficult to put into words. If you have difficulty expressing yourself in this way, look at some of the descriptions in the McGill Pain Questionnaire on page 136 and try to work out from them which is applicable to your type of pain.

When the doctor knows where the pain is, and what type of pain it is, he will try to discover whether it is constant, or variable: does it come in short bursts and, if so, are they caused by specific factors? If it is constant, is it worse at any particular time, such as in the evening, during the night, or first thing in the morning? Then, he will want to know what things make it worse, or better. Again, stick to significant points, not minutiae from several years ago.

If your GP is hearing about your chronic pain for the first time, he will probably already know something of your background. A hospital specialist, however, will probably need to find out a little more about you and your family and the effect the pain has had on your activities and your personality. For example, has it got you down or made you frustrated? Has it stopped you from sleeping? What other effects has it had on your life?

Following this, the doctor may carry out an examination. This is not always helpful in chronic pain; often, the history is the most relevant and will suggest the type of condition, or conditions, which are producing and maintaining the discomfort. However, a brief examination might show if there is any nerve involvement, or how much muscle spasm there is. Depending on the results of the examination, the doctor may decide to refer you for specialist investigations or tests.

Treatments available for chronic pain

In medicine, the main aim is to treat the underlying condition. It may be a sore throat from tonsillitis, cured when antibiotics kill the bacteria, or removing the appendix to relieve the pain of appendicitis.

However, for people with chronic pain, the underlying condition is obviously not treatable – at least, not to relieve their discomfort. Hence, pain clinics offer five different types of therapy to reduce discomfort. They try to select the most appropriate method, or methods, to help the chronic pain sufferer and then monitor the patient to see if the treatment is effective.

As it is unlikely that a cure will result, treatment is aimed at reducing the pain, increasing activity and improving the quality of life. The five types of therapy used are:

- Medical (drugs and medication)
- Surgical (which includes nerve blocks)
- Stimulation
- Physical
- Psychological

It is important to look at these in more detail:

Medications

These are so important that a chapter has been devoted to them. Generally, the rule is that non-addictive drugs can be used, as long as they do not produce side-effects. Addictive drugs, such as codeine, DF118 and Distalgesics, should only be used if the sufferer shows signs of increased activity when taking them.

There is a fine line between administering drugs to relieve pain and improving a patient's quality of life. High drug dosages may sedate someone, temporarily reduce pain and lessen the likelihood of them complaining, but they do not do them any service.

It is rather like the story of the camel's hump. A man who

thought camels looked uncomfortable with humps bred and cross-bred them until the hump had been eliminated. He was pleased with his work, until someone pointed out that he had certainly done an effective job – but they weren't camels anymore. Over-use of drugs may change someone's personality; they may not complain of pain, but they are no longer the same person.

Some time ago, lobotomy operations were carried out to reduce chronic pain by removing part of the frontal lobe of the brain. It changed the personality so much that they lost their awareness. The fact that they no longer seemed the same person upset their families. Medicine has since acquired more sophistication, but it only performs a useful function when the right outcome is achieved.

Surgical Treatments

Anaesthetists became involved in pain relief through their use of nerve blocks for the relief of post-operative pain. Because nerve blocks gave excellent results for short periods, surgeons and anaesthetists thought that more permanent blocks could achieve long-term results with chronic pain.

Severing or surgically damaging a nerve, however, leads to problems. One obvious drawback is that there is a loss of sensation and power and the patient may not be able to feel or move part of his body. However, some people would still trade this for pain relief.

Unfortunately, damage to the nerve tissue leads to changes in the central nervous system itself, with unpleasant consequences. The remaining fibres of a damaged pain nerve are still able to fire off warning messages to the brain that something is amiss, producing an unpleasant pain in a numb area. This is precisely what happens in conditions like shingles (post-herpetic neuralgia). It can occur either immediately following the block, or several months later.

Another problem with chronic pain is that most people experience pain over quite a wide area, supplied by many different nerves. Thus, many different procedures would have to be carried out, even to reduce the pain in the first place.

However, there are a few conditions in which nerve blocks can be very useful. These include certain types of cancer pain, in specific areas, and trigeminal neuralgia. This is a very painful condition of the face with intermittent, sharp, shooting pain triggered by light touch, a breath of wind or the motion of eating. This nerve is susceptible to blocking and a procedure is carried out to burn the nerve, which leaves part of the face numb, but does not produce any disfigurement and completely relieves the pain for long periods. It is only appropriate for trigeminal neuralgia and does not work for other types of facial pain.

Surgical treatment may also involve temporary nerve blocks being carried out. In many cases, they are diagnostic blocks, with local anaesthetic, to try and identify which group of nerves are causing the problem. In this way, the sympathetic nerves can be blocked off for a few hours and, if the pain is relieved, we know that the sympathetic nerves are causing it.

Specific spinal nerves can also be blocked, along with the nerves around the facet joints and the intercostal nerves below the ribs.

Alternatively, a differential spinal block might be tried. Usually, once the nerve is blocked off, and the pain is still felt, it indicates it is coming from somewhere else. In the case of a differential spinal block, if the pain is still present it indicates that it has now become central; some part of the brain is initiating the pain, even if it is felt in the back or the legs.

If you receive surgical injections you may be given therapeutic substances, such as steroids or cortisone, combined with local anaesthetic. Long-acting steroids can be injected into a joint or into the epidural space to produce an intense local anti-inflammatory effect, reducing the amount of pain and muscle spasm. The importance of this is not that it cures the condition, but that it might break the cycle of spasm and inactivity which keep the pain going. The pain sufferer will hopefully then be able to become more mobile and relaxed. In a few weeks or months, by the time the effect of the block wears off, the increased strength, mobility and flexibility of muscles will have taken over, affording less discomfort and the freedom to move more easily. Other drugs used in this way include Guanethidine to block the sympathetic nerves and Hyalase, sometimes used in our Pain Relief Unit to break down scar tissue.

Surgery

In the past, many types of surgery have been used on the spinal cord and the brain to try to relieve chronic pain. Unfortunately, the treatment sometimes appears to have been worse than the disease.

As described earlier, the frontal lobes of the brain used to be removed in the 1930s, in what turned out to be a mutilating operation which destroyed the patient's personality. This type of procedure is now condemned by most specialists. There are modifications of this type of surgery, however, which cause less damage, but they are very specialized and only useful in one or two rare conditions.

Operations can also be carried out on the spinal cord to relieve pain. One of them, the anterolateral cordotomy, interrupts the pain tracts in the spinal cord, but this is generally only used for cancer pain. The pituitary gland used to be surgically damaged for cancer as well, by inserting a needle through the nose into the pituitary and injecting alcohol, or other toxic substances. This technique has now been superceded by medication to achieve the same effect with less trauma. In general, surgery on the brain and the spinal cord to relieve pain is highly specialized and only appropriate in certain limited conditions.

Stimulation Techniques

Acupuncture has been used at Walton Hospital's Centre for Pain Relief since 1971 and is now such a standard technique in pain clinics that it is no longer considered 'alternative'. A description of acupuncture methods may be found in the chapter on Alternative Medicine.

Acupuncture stimulation seems to affect the spinal gate which selects the amount of pain messages passing through the

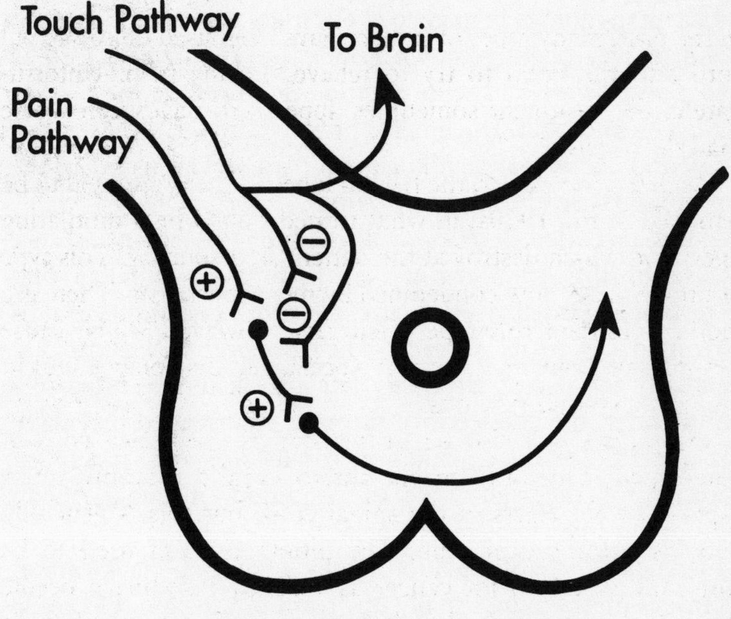

INHIBITORY EFFECT OF TOUCH ON PAIN

spinal cord on their way to the brain. Acupuncture is a high-intensity/low-frequency treatment – high-intensit because you know it is being done and it can even be slightly unpleasant; low-frequency because stimulations are about two per second.

Another form of electrical stimulation is Transcutaneous Nerve Stimulation (known as TENS). This is low-intensity (it doesn't hurt and produces just a tingling sensation) and high-frequency (stimulation is about 100 times per second). When the gate control theory was published by Melzack and Wall in 1965, it was realized that electricity had a part to play in reducing pain. If touch fibres could be stimulated, the resulting messages passing into the spinal cord would 'jam' the pain messages. Input of this type actually seemed to close the pain gate.

Like many things in medicine, electrical nerve stimulation is a re-discovery of long-known principles. The ancient Greeks used a similar method with electric eels to relieve the pain of headaches and gout. Documents prepared by the physicians of the period show that significant care was taken to select the appropriate type of fish for the pain.

Hand-generated electricity was used to relieve pain and cure disease in the 19th century. It became so popular that Victorians regarded it as a cure-all, and exaggerated claims were made as to its efficacy. They became so bizarre that eventually the use of electricity fell into disrepute. Almost a century later, the gate control theory demonstrated that there was a physiological explanation for its use and, if applied correctly for the right type of condition, it might be an appropriate and harmless treatment.

Electrical Nerve Stimulation works by placing black carbon electrodes on the skin, usually upstream of the pain. Electrode jelly, or jelly pads, are used to ensure good contact and to avoid burning the skin. A current is generated from a battery-powered unit, which produces tingling sensations on the skin beneath the pads and sometimes spreads between the pads. For the best result, the tingling must mix in with the pain and produce a pleasant substitute for it.

Pain clinics often instruct patients in the use of these machines and may loan them a unit for a time. As they cost in the region of £80 upwards and help only 30 to 40 per cent of people who have them, an impulse purchase is not recommended. In any event, the best results come from being taught how to use the machine properly by someone familiar with them. In general, the more time and effort that is spent working with the machine, the more likely it is that good results will ensue.

Different forms of stimulation may be applied with the machine to discover which is most effective. Trial and error reveals the most beneficial position of the pads and, obviously, the pain area needs to be fairly localized to give the technique a chance to work. Total body pain is unlikely to be helped by TENS.

If two or three different areas are affected, then many units contain two pairs of leads, so that different areas may be treated simultaneously. Providing that plenty of jelly is used, and the pads are not left on for too long, equipment from reputable companies is quite safe. (Some new electrodes are self adhesive and require no jelly.) The pads should not be used in the neck region, or if the patient has a pacemaker.

The equipment should also not be used if you drive or operate machinery, at least not until you have had a great deal of experience with TENS. Movement is likely to make the pads shift position, causing a surge of electricity which might produce a sharp sensation, making you jump or lose concentration! However, many patients who are familiar with the system are able to use the machines to increase their activity, including driving.

Some patients with TENS machines say that they help up to

a point, but do not feel that they are powerful enough, or do not reach a wide enough area. It may be suitable for these people to have an implanted dorsal column stimulator. This is an electrode, implanted surgically in the epidural space, near to the spinal cord. A receiver left under the skin picks up signals using a box similar to the TENS machine, and an aerial. This is a rather hi-tech form of treatment and only suitable for certain types of pain, and certain types of people. It needs to be evaluated very carefully before being used.

Electrodes can even be implanted in the brain to stimulate relevant areas, in the hope of leading to a reduction in pain messages. This technique is clearly even more potentially dangerous than dorsal column stimulation. It is not particularly favoured in Britain, but has proved popular in parts of the USA. A very thorough assessment of the likelihood of success has to be made before embarking on this expensive and time-consuming method of treatment.

It should be noted that all of these stimulation techniques involve co-operation from the patient and TENS, in particular, is very much a self-help operation. None of them actually remove the pain altogether, but reduce it to more bearable levels. All of them depend on the pain sufferer using this respite to increase activity, with subsequent improvement to his well-being, reduction in muscle spasm and a return to a more normal lifestyle.

Physical Treatments

These include all of the physiotherapy treatments many chronic pain sufferers may have had, as well as manipulation, which is dealt with under Osteopathy and Chiropractic in the next chapter.

Vibration, local massage and application of heat and cold have all been used to try to reduce chronic pain. Like many treatments, they often have a part to play in cutting down pain, but all depend very much on the patient's personal response. In our experience, none of them work with passive people who are not prepared to do something for themselves. Any that help, however, are worthwhile considering, in conjunction with the self-help techniques outlined in this book.

Psychological Techniques

Hypnosis is now used quite regularly by doctors and can be useful for chronic pain, though the effect tends to wear off. Biofeedback is popular in America and has been used to treat a wide variety of pain syndromes. The most common technique is to use a device which measures muscle tension, with a dial or indicator that the patient can watch. He is then encouraged to relax his muscles and observe the results. Usually, more muscle tension is produced on the first attempt until, with practice, better relaxation is achieved. The name comes from the 'feedback' of a biological measurement.

Cognitive therapy studies the patient's thoughts and feelings about pain and tries to influence them. For example, sufferers are encouraged to think of their pain as a sensation, to realize that it is not harmful or dangerous, and to gain a measure of control. Techniques such as these are clearly helpful to any form of self-help programme.

Behavioural Therapy concentrates not on the pain, but what the patient does when the pain is felt. The method has been used in the USA for 20 years or more and is often a fairly tough programme. The therapist draws up written contracts with the patient specifying goals the patient wishes to achieve, what he will have to do to achieve them and what the staff will do to assist.

Steps are taken to withdraw medication and any exhibitions of pain behaviour are ignored. Patients' families are also involved and taught to reinforce healthy behaviour and to ignore pain behaviour. Pure behavioural programmes of this kind are now quite rare, although elements of them have become an important part of many treatment regimes and self-help programmes.

Many of the treatments described are offered only after being referred for more specialized therapy by your local GP. Many doctors do not understand the complexities and ramifications of chronic pain and feel daunted by the prospect of long-term patients who visit them again and again in the hope of relieving their condition.

It is important to maintain a good relationship with your doctor or specialist to ensure that you get the right treatment for your condition. Chronic pain patients who devote their lives to searching for a cure waste energy which could be put to more profitable use helping themselves.

If, for example, you visit an orthopaedic surgeon who specializes in back problems often enough, and insist for long enough, you are likely to have a second operation. To someone who has a hammer, the saying goes, everything looks like a nail. Despite the fact that there is only a one per cent chance of further back operations being successful, you may nevertheless force the specialist into it in the hope of being part of the fortunate one per cent.

If the operation only makes the problem worse, and you are one of the 99 per cent, you will obviously not be very happy. Neither, to an extent, will the surgeon but, at least he will have fulfilled his contract and discharged his responsibility. He may have hammered your nail, but it has done no good whatsoever.

A dentist friend had a patient who constantly complained about an aching tooth. The dentist did not want to take it out because it appeared to be quite healthy. He worried that, if he removed the tooth, the pain would probably be worse, but the patient insisted. Finally, he gave in and took the tooth out. The result, predictably, was that the pain increased. The dentist extracted the tooth because the patient pressured him so much that, eventually, he would have probably agreed to anything to get rid of the patient.

The same applies to prescriptions. You know that prolonged use of drugs is not good for you but, when your body demands drugs, you need to obtain them without feeling bad about it. Many chronic pain patients have a conversation with their GP which goes something like this:

Patient: 'I don't want to take drugs, but the pain is terrible.'
Doctor: 'I'm sorry, but if that's what you want, there's nothing I can do. You'll have to cope with it.'
Patient: 'I can't possibly cope with it. It's awful.'
Doctor: 'I can give you some tablets that might help.'
Patient: 'They were wonderful last time I had them. Thank you.'

The doctor makes out the prescription and the patient tells his family and friends: 'I didn't want to take drugs, but the doctor made me.'

If you keep in mind what will genuinely help you to overcome your pain, and phrase your questions intelligently, you will get the best from your doctor. However, if you use your five minute appointment to complain and pester him about your pain, he will inevitably give you drugs and advise you to rest. This, of course, is the wrong approach to chronic pain but the fault probably lies more with the way that you framed the question than with your doctor.

If you say: 'Look, doctor, we both know I'm in pain, but I want to lead a better life. I don't want to take tablets and I don't want to give up exercise. Is it safe to carry on?', he will be understanding and sympathetic. Ultimately, your doctor wants to do the best he can for you. If you force him to do otherwise, he will capitulate because he has a waiting room full of other patients who require his attention.

Pressing for what you, or your subconscious, regards as the easy way out is not necessarily best for you, physically or emotionally.

It is not unusual for patients to say: 'I've been doing my exercises every day, doctor, but that particular one is really too painful. I can't manage it.' They phrase it this way, hoping to hear me sympathize and advise them to drop the exercise in question. To their great disappointment, I encourage them to carry on and try to break through the emotional barrier because we both know that, for chronic pain patients, hurt does not mean harm.

Using your doctor wisely means being honest with him, not using him for an ulterior motive. He is on your side but, if the meeting becomes a contest of wills and you pressure him into a position which is against your best interests, your relationship will deteriorate.

By the time your next appointment comes around, there is every likelihood that your discomfort will have increased and your doctor will get the blame. Dissatisfaction leads to doctor-shopping which, long-term, will only prolong pain, not reduce it.

9

Alternative medicine

Despite increased amounts spent on the National Health Service every year, people are turning to alternative medicine in greater numbers. Doctors have also become more aware that certain techniques play a part in helping people with illness. Some therapies, once on the fringe of established medicine, have now become accepted into the fold and can hardly be thought of as 'alternative' at all.

Relaxation techniques and hypnotherapy are today commonplace in psychiatric units and pain relief centres. Acupuncture certainly causes less rising of the hackles among elderly consultants than it used to. Aromatherapy, osteopathy and chiropractics, too, scarcely raise an eyebrow among BMA members, where once they produced snorts of outrage.

So, why are more and more ordinary people seeking out alternative remedies for their illnesses? On the surface, it might be thought to indicate that modern medicine is not effective, but this is patently not true. Modern drugs and surgery are becoming more accurate with fewer side-effects and higher success rates every year. People do worry about the side-effects of medicines and surgery and the medical profession takes note of their views and tries to improve the quality of life of patients, as well as reducing their suffering.

Perhaps the answer is that people have a greater expectation of good health. Certainly, increasing numbers expect their doctor to listen to accounts of their symptoms and provide something to relieve the burden of their illness.

This is understandable in a world where TV advertisements assure us that there is no need to suffer headaches because Drug X will magic them away, or hay fever can be banished by Drug Y, without ill effects. Advances in medicine tend to be reported sensationally with little attention to the small print of the research, or any side-effects a new treatment might bring. Increased leisure may have given us more time to think about our bodies, but perhaps we worship them too much, without putting in the time and effort to keep them in good condition.

Many folk remedies have been around for thousands of years, and have been used by the general population for centuries, the only change being that they have perhaps become more formalized. Once, someone may have consulted their corner shop chemist, or the wise old woman down the street, for a non-specific remedy. Now, they are more likely to have heard of the chap across town who practices Rolfing, or the woman 200 miles away with a reputation in radionics.

How effective are alternative remedies and, more importantly, do they actually work? Obviously, some achieve better results than others and several different factors have to be considered.

With any form of therapy there is a placebo effect, which comes from the Latin *placere*, 'to please' ('placebo' means literally 'I will please'). From time to time, any normal person may experience the placebo effect and patients sometimes improve despite a lack of any active treatment. If patients recovering from surgery were told that they were going to be given a new drug, flown in from Italy, and that it gave the finest pain control since morphine, it would be reasonable to expect between 30 to 40 per cent to experience good pain relief after the injection and remain comfortable for some hours. The substance administered could be little more than sterile water.

Obviously, some inert treatments offered to patients will have the effect of making them feel better, even if they contain no active ingredient. It might even be argued that this doesn't matter, providing they have the desired effect.

If someone with severe arthritis visits his doctor wearing a copper bracelet and says that the pain has completely disappeared, the doctor would be foolish to put him down. His wisest answer would be: 'Wonderful – as long as it works for you, keep wearing the bracelet.' The doctor is hardly likely to recommend bracelets to his other hundred arthritis patients, as some might demand a more scientific approach to their problem.

Of course, the alternative therapy being used may have a genuine effect. Some alternative treatments undoubtedly go beyond the placebo and it is reasonable that they have been harnessed within the Health Service to try to reduce symptoms with a minimum of side-effects. It would take a very hard-nosed scientist indeed to claim that no alternative therapies ever had a therapeutic effect beyond placebos. Most researchers freely admit that there is a lot more to nature than we know at present; that science has only begun to scrape the surface of the world about us and that natural phenomena do occur.

One advantage alternative medicine practitioners have is more time to spend with their patients than the average hard-pressed GP or hospital doctor. The old saying 'Time is a great healer' is particularly appropriate when half the battle is airing your symptoms to someone who listens and cares.

People who practise alternative medicine also dispense sound advice: an acupuncture treatment may be combined with a recommendation to exercise daily; spiritual healing may contain messages to sort out your problems; aromatherapy may be given with advice to spend half an hour each day relaxing.

This kind of time spent listening to the patient was one of the attributes of the old-fashioned family doctor, in the days when it was described as 'bedside manner'. In many instances, this was all he had, as medicines in the last century were generally quite dismal and many have long since been discontinued. Some of the therapies available plainly did more harm than good and it is surprising that patients survived in spite of them.

Doctors today have a wide variety of treatments at their fingertips, but more patients to attend to and less time to spend with them. In many ways the alternative therapist has taken over the old role of listener and counsellor.

Naturally, there will also always be people for whom nothing is really worthwhile unless you have to pay for it. The problem with some repetitive alternative therapies is that you certainly do have to pay for them. In some cases, the best private hospital at £400 might be considerably cheaper.

The fact remains that some advice is only readily taken when it is paid for. A story illustrating this is that of a mother in her early 40s suffering from abdominal pain. The local specialist made a domiciliary visit and, being a somewhat busy and rather terse man, muttered that it was only an irritable bowel. He told her that she should consider herself lucky to have a good family and should get on with everyday living.

The family did not take kindly to this advice and went back to their GP, demanding to see the finest consultant that money could buy. Two days later the great man, a Knight of the Realm, swept up the drive in his Rolls. He listened gravely to the woman's story, carried out a thorough examination and drew up a plan of action.

The son was instructed to open all the windows for half an hour every morning and every afternoon. The eldest daughter was ordered to shoulder the burden of the housework and the youngest told to read to her mother for 45 minutes each day. The husband was taken aside and advised to shout less and work harder. Granny had to prepare wholesome soups and make sure the patient took them.

As far as the abdominal complaint was concerned, there was no effective treatment, and none was offered. The family, however felt delighted with the visit and, when his account for £150 arrived, considered it money well spent. The family buckled to and felt much improved because they had paid for sound advice.

Alternative medicine has both advantages and disadvantages. On the credit side, it is claimed that it does little harm and, largely, this is true. It also benefits the patient to have a positive outlook and some optimism about the future. The practitioner spends time with the sufferer, good advice may be given and touch is often used to make the patient feel cared for. Above all, of course, there is the potential for genuine action and results.

The downside is that any active treatment carries potential harm. Even innocent herbs such as parsley can cause haemorrhage in over-dosage. Acupuncture placed unskilfully around the chest could produce a pneumothorax, or punctured lung, while unsterile needles carry an obvious risk of hepatitis or AIDS. Another possible negative effective might include a patient abandoning conventional therapies because he has total belief in alternative therapy and wishes to avoid any unpleasant side-effects of his medication. Any initial sense of well-being might unfortunately mask a realization that his condition is worsening, until it is too late.

Commencing any new treatment can produce optimism and positive thoughts about the future, but an awareness that it is not working may lead to deepening depression and feelings of despair, with hope of a cure dashed once more.

The potential cost of long-term, ongoing alternative therapy should also be considered, whether or not it is helping. Sixteen treatments may solve the therapist's problem (i.e. his bank balance) but prove to be the straw that broke the camel's back for the chronic invalid without adequate sources of income because of his condition.

The intention here is not to dissuade anyone from seeking alternative help, but to consider its disadvantages and pitfalls. Perhaps the most important aspect of the debit side to consider is that someone who pursues alternative treatment in the hope of a cure might be tempted to disregard important self-help techniques which are essential to his improvement.

In 1983, the British Medical Association set up a study of alternative medicines to assess whether they had any true value beyond the placebo effect. The Committee concluded that the popularity of alternative treatments suggested that conventional medicine was obviously lacking – particularly in time devoted to patients and explaining to them, reducing side-effects of drugs and in improving the quality of life. However, they did not gather enough evidence to prove beyond all doubt that alternative therapies had an inherent action.

Among their conclusions, they noted numerous reports from people of help from acupuncture, osteopathy and chiropractic and felt that relaxation techniques, such as hypnotherapy and biofeedback, were well worthwhile. Herbal remedies, of course, have been around for thousands of years and purified forms are still used in the treatment of many conditions.

To help guide you through the maze – and minefield – of alternative medicine, here is a directory of treatments recommended for use in chronic pain, with comments on their efficacy and drawbacks:

Acupressure

A mixture of massage and acupuncture. Instead of piercing the skin with needles, practitioners use thumb and fingertip massage to put pressure on acupuncture points. There are different schools of acupressure, including Shiatsu.

Local stimulation of pressure points can make some painful conditions worse, due to painful nodules in the muscles. On the whole, acupressure is either harmless, or might do quite an amount of good. If three or four treatments fail to help, it is unlikely that further therapy will be useful. If one treatment makes you worse, then it would be best to abandon it.

One of the great potential benefits of acupressure is that, if it does help, chronic pain sufferers can stimulate the points themselves, or get a friend or member of the family to help them.

Acupuncture

This ancient Chinese method of treatment has been around for three or four thousand years. The word comes from *acus*, 'a needle' and *punctura*, 'to prick'. It is thought to have originated when it was noticed that soldiers wounded in battle with arrows and spears appeared to feel less pain than the extent of their injuries suggested. In addition, they sometimes recovered from other ailments.

Treatments were refined over the years by trial and error before acupuncture arrived at its present form. It was introduced to the West by a 17th century Dutch physician and, in 1823, *The Lancet* reported its successful use in treating rheumatism. Acupuncture's popularity in Britain revived with the opening-up of China to British physicians in the early 1970s, when many observed its use as an anaesthetic and pain-relieving agent.

It was first used at Walton's Pain Relief Clinic in 1971 and has been used on a regular basis ever since.

Acupuncture points are stimulated with needles, either twiddled by the fingers, or by means of a lead clipped to the needle, which is then stimulated by an electro-acupuncture device. Laser acupuncture has also been used, but it is our opinion at the Pain Relief Clinic that this is a placebo and lacks the inherent physical action of the use of needles.

The Chinese believe that there is a balance in the body between *Yin* and *Yang* and that there are fourteen meridians extending like trunk roads over the body, each linking acupuncture points.

Acupuncturists follow different schools of diagnosis and treatment but the method is usually the same – a very fine needle inserted into the relevant points and twisted. There is a slight prick when the needle goes in. Stimulation of the needle produces a heavy numbness, or tingling sensation, which can be quite marked at times.

Modern scientists believe that this stimulation produces activity in rapidly-acting pain fibres, resulting in the release of endorphins, the body's natural pain killers.

There is also good evidence to suggest that acupuncture therapy promotes the release of steroids, which can also have a beneficial effect on many painful conditions.

Acupuncture can certainly have a part to play in the relief of chronic pain. But, again, if two or three treatments produce no response, then it is not worth persevering with. A reputable therapist should be found, once your GP has confirmed that there are no untoward consequences in blocking off any pain.

The Alexander Technique

Developed by an Australian actor, F.M. Alexander, and based on his supposition that many conditions could be relieved by improving posture. This certainly seems a sensible idea and there are several books available on the Alexander Technique and many registered practitioners (see the back of this book for a contact address).

As long as you can afford it, it would seem reasonable to consult an Alexander Technique teacher in the first instance, then build up your own exercises, as advised by him and supported by any books available.

Sometimes, the Technique is a little over-sold by practitioners, who claim it can achieve almost anything. However, it is worth remembering that most patients with chronic pain tend to have very poor posture and improving this is likely to have a beneficial effect. The method is best used in conjunction with relaxation training, appropriate targeting and positive thinking techniques.

Aromatherapy

This consists of using highly-concentrated and scented plant oils and, like many alternative therapies, has probably existed for thousands of years. Any visit to a place like The Body Shop will provide many of the essential oils necessary for treatment.

It is best to get someone else to massage them in, though they can also be inhaled or added to a hot bath. Eucalyptus is said to be good for headaches and muscular pain; juniper for arthritis, marjoram for migraine and cramp; and Roman camomile for headaches. Many oils are also recommended for relaxation.

There is no scientific evidence that any one oil is more effective than another, but most patients find aromatherapy treatment positive and beneficial and it has been used on patients on the Pain Management Programme. It should be stressed, however, that this is part of a programme and not a passive treatment which allows the sufferer to lie down and be cured without any effort on his part. We allow aromatherapy as a reward after patients have achieved targets in physical therapy, or to help relaxation in the early stages. If used in this way it should certainly be of positive benefit.

Auricular Therapy

A form of acupuncture, often practised by many general acupuncturists. Therapists believe that each part of the body is represented by a point on the ear and various conditions can be improved by stimulating the relevant point with an acupuncture needle, or a small tack, or press needle, taped in position in the ear.

There is no evidence that the treatment is any better than acupuncture. A potential advantage is that, if a press-stud is used, the patient can stimulate the point himself between visits to the acupuncturist, perhaps intensifying the treatment and reducing cost.

Autogenic Training

A series of six mental exercises used to relieve stress and help the body to cure itself. In some ways, autogenic training is similar to meditation and yoga. As relaxation is helpful for chronic pain, it has been used successfully for many people with backache, migraine and irritable bowel syndrome.

It is also useful in sympathetic nerve over-activity and is now so accepted by doctors that it can hardly be called 'alternative'. However, it should be again stressed that it is unlikely to make everybody with chronic pain completely better, unless used in conjunction with other therapies.

Ayurvedic Medicine

The main form of medicine in India, where it is used alongside orthodox techniques. Its aim is mainly prevention and people keep in touch with their therapist who monitors their lifestyle and tries to steer them from bad habits which produce illness.

When illness does occur, a wide variety of treatments are used, from herbs to mineral supplements, as well as dietary regimes, massage and relaxation. It adds up to a fairly complete way of life which, consequently, is rather difficult for Westerners to adopt if they have been chronically ill for some time. Much of it is common sense and would undoubtedly form the basis of an excellent Indian-style pain management programme.

Bach Remedies

A form of homeopathy popularized by an English physician named Dr Edward Bach. Thirty eight preparations are made from wild flowers and plants, floated on spring water in sunlight. Chemical analysis of the remedies shows only spring water, with some alcohol. Consequently, most scientists do not accept that there is anything beyond a placebo effect when they produce benefit.

Biofeedback

The technique is now so widely used in America that it can no longer be regarded as alternative. The patient is taught to control his own body functions by receiving feedback from a machine which monitors the results of his efforts. Thus, the skin blood flow in the finger increases as the person becomes more relaxed and blood pressure drops.

Biofeedback can be a very useful way of helping pain. Unfortunately, it is time-consuming and therefore not widely available through the National Health Service.

Chiropractic

A form of treatment started by a magnetic healer named Daniel Palmer, in 1895. Scientific trials have shown that manipulation by a qualified practitioner is more effective than physiotherapy in back pain and is certainly worthwhile trying in musculo-skeletal pains of any description.

Chiropractors use X-rays to make diagnoses. The only quibble of medical practitioners is that they tend to dramatize the underlying problem, saying, for instance, that bones are out of place and need to be manipulated back into position.

It is certainly worthwhile visiting a chiropractor, having treatment and repeating it if there is benefit. However, do not attach too much weight to the explanation of the cause of your condition. By all means, carry out advice to increase your activity, change your lifestyle and relax muscles, which chiropractors are very skilled in communicating, in addition to their helpful manipulations.

Colour Therapy

There is little doubt that colour affects mood, but colour therapists believe that specific ailments can be cured by adjusting the colour input into the body. They may use Kirlian photography to capture the aura of electromagnetism around the body. Treatment consists of coloured lights being shone on the patient for about 20 minutes daily.

Colour therapy has been used for migraine and various forms of back pain, but it unlikely that it has any inherent value, apart from its effect on mood, relaxation and the placebo response. It is, however, unlikely to be harmful.

Copper Therapy

Wearing a copper bracelet is often cited as a way of reducing arthritic pain. Some studies claim that a remarkable number of pain sufferers are helped in this way, in the belief that traces of copper from the bracelet penetrate the skin. There is no scientific basis to this contention, but it is certainly a very cheap and harmless method of treatment. Any patient it works for is encouraged to continue its use.

Electrotherapy

The most useful form of this is the Transcutaneous Electrical Nerve Stimulator, described in the previous chapter. These are readily available at most pain clinics and should be used in conjunction with medical advice.

There is no place for exaggerated claims, occasionally reported in the Sunday papers, and units should not be bought without a reasonable trial period. There is little advantage in paying more than £100 per unit and they should be manufactured to approved safety standards.

Feldenkrais Method

A fairly recent method of self-help developed by Moshi Feldenkrais who used the technique to cure his own knee pain and went on to help family and friends. Others have now been taught how to use the method which helps people to understand how they move and improves their way of moving.

Sessions improve posture, reduce pain in muscles and increase the ability to relax. They also allow an increased range of movement and break the spasm-pain cycle. There are obvious similarities with the Alexander Technique and with T'ai Chi. Once again, the idea of gentle exercise, relaxation, improving posture and positive thinking are very similar to a pain management programme.

Herbal medicine

Herbal medicines have been around for thousands of years and some have been purified and adopted by the medical profession as the cornerstone of treatment for certain conditions. The foxglove yields digitalis, which is used for heart failure. From the poppy comes morphine and codeine – still the standard pain killers for post-operative pain and pain arising from heart attack and cancer. A form of aspirin comes from willow bark.

It has been estimated that 15 per cent of medication prescribed by GPs is plant-based. Throughout the world, herbal medicine is four times as commonly used as conventional medicine. Both in India (Ayurvedic medicine) and in China, herbal medicine is considered orthodox and dispensed in most hospitals.

Herbalists claim that their medication helps many long-standing conditions, such as arthritis and migraine. In addition, the herbalist might also suggest manipulations such as those performed by an osteopath. Medicines, creams or ointments might be prescribed, which are generally naturally-grown preparations of whole plants.

This is where herbal therapy diverges from modern medical opinion: in conventional medicine the active ingredient is identified, purified and served up in exact doses of medication; with herbal medicine, one can never be certain of the exact dose and the plant may contain additional substances which may, or may not, be useful.

Like all drugs, herbs are not completely safe. Lavender is said to be good for headaches and rheumatism and mint is also effective for headaches and stress. Most commonly available herbal remedies are harmless and research into the properties of exotic compounds now being discovered in the Amazonian jungle may well produce new drugs.

Healing

Sometimes called spiritual healing, this old-established technique has been used through the ages. There are now more than 20,000 healers practising in Britain, many of whom are registered with the Confederation of Healing Organisations, which has an approved code of conduct and training programme. Healers should always be selected from the Confederation.

A multitude of different techniques are used and they can often be dramatic. Many healers do not charge a fee, but ask for a donation. Full-time professional healers may charge £15 a session and more than this should be regarded with suspicion.

The medical profession generally takes the view that healers produce a form of placebo response in the patient. Competent healers who produce good results have a great deal of personal charisma. They are usually very relaxed and encourage positive thinking. We have used a healer in conjunction with the Walton Pain Management Programme for some time. Helen Yaffe-Smith has given her time freely over this period and feels she can help people, irrespective of whether they believe in her or have any personal religion. At times she can undoubtedly help patients to make dramatic breakthroughs in what they can do, or in their understanding of themselves. In this way, in conjunction with the Programme, it seems an excellent form of therapy.

As yet, there is no great body of evidence to suggest that healers can provide anyone with more than a 'good bedside manner', but studies continue to investigate the phenomenon, with interesting results. In general, healing can be useful for helping chronic pain and producing positive thinking – as long as the patient's hopes are not dashed if treatment is unsuccessful and sessions do not cost them too much. But beware of over-dramatic or manipulative therapists or groups.

Homeopathy

Homeopathy was developed by a German physician who believed that naturally-occurring substances which could produce symptoms would be able to treat the same symptoms if greatly diluted. Plant and mineral substances are most widely used, soaked in alcohol then diluted to prepare the homeopathic remedy. Arnica and Ipecacuanha are used for back pain and Pulsatilla for headache. Poison Ivy extract is recommended for arthritis, backache, sciatica and sprains, as well as depression! Homeopathy is available through the NHS and there are some homeopathic hospitals. The Queen Mother is a staunch supporter of homeopathic remedies and treatments can be bought in health food stores and chemists' shops.

Most doctors point out that little scientific research has been done to show that a homeopathic remedy is any better than an inert substance, such as boiled water. It is difficult to believe that preparations so dilute actually contain any active ingredients, but the preparations are also so dilute that they can do no harm. However, it is advisable to consult a qualified homeopath in the first place before undertaking a course of treatment. Then if a patient wants to take homeopathic remedies in conjunction with reducing intake of potentially troublesome conventional medicine, this is only to be encouraged.

Hydrotherapy

Some NHS hospitals offer hydrotherapy in the Physiotherapy Department. Spas are available throughout the world to help people with chronic disease or to relax and reinvigorate a jaded body. A warm bath is universally helpful to many people with chronic pain. Light exercise in water, with the support and buoyancy it gives the body, is usually well-tolerated even by quite infirm people.

Patients on the Pain Management Programme are encouraged to swim and exercise in water, though a significant number are nervous of water and find themselves unable to use this useful form of therapy.

Hydrotherapy must be considered as part of a general regime of increasing fitness and producing relaxation. Any hydrotherapist chosen should be carefully screened to ensure their experience and qualifications. Changing from hot to cold baths should be done with care. The general rule is, if you don't fancy the treatment, don't have it.

Hypnotherapy

Franz Mesmer, an 18th century Austrian doctor, popularized mesmerism, which developed into hypnotism. Anyone can call themselves a hypnotist, but there are highly-trained therapists who can undoubtedly produce quite dramatic effects in a hypnotic subject. Once the therapist has induced a trance-like state, positive suggestions are given. It is thought that these go directly into the subconscious, which has the ability to do a great deal of positive good to the body, if it wishes.

Someone successfully hypnotized can have their pain reduced by a very significant degree, although this belief does not always last once the trance is over. For pain, it is better if subjects are taught self-hypnosis so that they can help themselves in the future. Hypnotherapy is not usually offered through the NHS. It has to be sought as a private treatment and can be quite expensive.

Hypnosis is without doubt a powerful tool. It can be effectively used for chronic pain, but is very time-consuming as a treatment. Most doctors share the experience that hypnosis can work at first, but that the effect wears off with time. To maintain it, the subject often needs to continue to work for a considerable period every day, either with the hypnotist at increasing expense, or with self-hypnosis. On the whole, hypnosis is safe, as long as used by a bona fide practitioner. The address of the British Society for Medical and Dental Hypnosis can be found at the back of the book.

Kirlian Photography

This therapy consists of photographs taken of the subject, or specific areas of the body, to reveal the electromagnetic field around the area. This is used as a diagnostic tool and a variety of treatments are then instituted in an effort to make the photograph more 'normal'. Pictures produced are certainly dramatic, but they are clearly not a reliable means of diagnosis. Some patients become alarmed at suggestions made by practitioners about the underlying cause of their condition which sometimes are very inaccurate. For diagnosis, it is better to stick to a qualified doctor.

Massage

Massage has been practised for more than 5,000 years and takes many different forms which can be helpful in relieving pain and tension. It does not actually cure any condition but, obviously, if it makes the patient feel better, it is doing some good. A qualified masseur should be found and this might become expensive.

It is perfectly reasonable to attend classes given by someone with experience and then give, or receive, the treatment with a partner or close friend. It is important to use massage as part of a rehabilitation regime, rather than passively accepting that massage alone will make you better. If any massage techniques prove to be particularly painful, they should be avoided.

Meditation

Another ancient form of therapy, used in the East for thousands of years. Yoga grew from meditation and, over the years, various schools of meditation have evolved, some of which often argue about the 'right' method. The general aim is to achieve a tranquil state of mind and some doctors see it as akin to self-hypnosis, or deep relaxation. If not too much time or money is devoted to its pursuit, it can become a useful part of coping with pain.

Osteopathy

Originated by an American doctor in the late 19th century to diagnose and treat mechanical problems in the body. As these are a common cause of chronic pain, it is obviously worthwhile investigating. There is a register of qualified osteopaths, and practitioners have to undergo a four-year degree course at an osteopathic college.

Treatment usually involves manipulation of the affected part of the body. Many people benefit from osteopathy, though over-zealous manipulation of a painful area can make things temporarily worse. As in all things, choose your osteopath wisely and take stock of how you are progressing after a short course of treatment. If there seems to be improvement, continue.

Osteopathy often appears to be useful for acute conditions, but the problem in chronic pain is that any useful response to treatment is seldom long-lived. Treatment needs to be repeated at regular intervals and the beneficial effect may even fade with time.

Radionics

Radionics is a method of distant healing in which the patient never need actually see the therapist. The patient fills in a case history form and sometimes sends skin scrapings, or a lock of hair for the practitioner to analyse before remitting treatments through the ether. No studies have been made which suggest there is anything more to this than a placebo effect. In general, doctors feel that the time, energy and money spent could be better invested elsewhere.

Reflexology

Rather like auricular therapy, reflexologists use charts of the feet which represent all parts of the body. Massage of the appropriate zone is supposed to clear energy channels, thus allowing the body to heal. Reflexology has been used for many years in conjunction with acupressure, but was popularized by an American surgeon, Dr Fitzgerald, at the turn of the century.

Reflexologists undoubtedly have the ability to relax some people, but it is unlikely that the treatment has any inherent effect on pain beyond this. Some practitioners make extravagant and worrying claims that the patient has hitherto undiagnosed illnesses, which can only be improved by a long, and expensive, course of treatment. If reflexology is required, members of the British Reflexology Association should be sought.

Rolfing

A recent development which involves massage and mild manipulation. Improving posture and reducing muscle spasm are obviously useful and there are similarities between Rolfing and the Alexander Technique combined with massage.

Shiatsu

A specific form of massage, practised in Japan. It is similar in some ways to acupressure and, providing a bona fide therapist is used, can be of benefit in many painful conditions. It should obviously not be used if it produces a significant increase in pain, or if there is no improvement within a few sessions.

Sound Therapy

This may vary from the use of electronic waves directed at the body, to chanting and singing. Ultrasound is, of course, a conventional physiotherapy technique, while chanting is part of many meditation techniques. There does not seem to be any inherent effect beyond the use these techniques might already have.

T'ai Chi

A form of flowing movements, combined with relaxation and meditation techniques, developed in China in the 11th century. Each individual movement is fairly easy, but requires good balance, flexibility and relaxation. The movements are very exact and require a great deal of concentration.

People of any age can try T'ai Chi, although those with chronic pain find the balance and flexibility difficult to begin with. Great benefit can be obtained from gradual progression. T'ai Chi has been taught at the Pain Management Programme for the past eight years and a significant number of chronic pain sufferers have benefited tremendously from continued practice. It is certainly well worth trying for anyone in chronic pain, even though not everyone will appreciate the philosophy behind it, or be able to carry out some of the more difficult movements.

Visualization Therapy

This treatment is based upon the therapist asking you to imagine a scene in your mind's eye, related to your problem. If, for example, you have back pain, you might be asked to imagine your spine as a tree, and then describe what the tree looks like. You might see it as withered or lightning-struck and the therapist will encourage you to change it into a young sapling, gradually growing straight and strong and in full health.

This technique is used by many alternative therapists, especially those working on relaxation methods. It is also used by our own healer, as well as our psychologists. Visualization is a reasonable way of producing relaxation and reinforces the positive thinking we try to teach. If you can't see yourself as healthy, it is difficult to become healthy.

Yoga

Yoga takes many different forms. Hatha Yoga, for instance, concentrates on postures, while Raja Yoga focuses on mental control. In the past 30 years it has become extremely popular in the UK. A combination of exercise, flexibility and relaxation is what we are trying to develop in chronic pain sufferers, anyway. As long as the postures are not overdone, it can be very useful for people with chronic pain.

There are a great variety of yoga teachers, some perhaps a little too insistent on exercise, and some undoubtedly a little weird, but most people can find someone with whom they feel comfortable. Practised in a group, it can be an enjoyable way to improve your health.

These are the most commonly used alternative techniques which have been recommended for chronic pain. There are also many good books on alternative medicine – we would recommend Michael Murray's and Joseph Pizzorno's *The Encyclopaedia of Natural Medicine* published by Optima and the Reader's Digest *Family Guide To Alternative Medicine* by Dr Pietroni.

Many of the techniques emphasize self-help through relaxation and exercise. Precise posture is also important, along with positive thinking. Providing you find a reputable practitioner and the technique seems to be helping without any side-effects and, if you realize that it is not a cure but a means of reducing your symptoms and increasing activity, then alternative therapy can only be of positive benefit.

10

Keeping it going

After reading this book, or attending a Pain Management Programme, you will hopefully feel inspired to continue to fight to reduce your pain to an acceptable level. Keeping the momentum going on your own is not easy and group activities, such as those of SHIP (Self Help In Pain) may provide valuable encouragement and support.

In addition, there are tried and tested guidelines which can help prevent a slide back into old pain behaviour. Adhering to them means increasing your chances of a return to normal life. At Walton Hospital's Pain Management Programme, patients are given a lecture on Dr Chris Wells's Ten Commandments of personal pain management before leaving the course to return home.

Some patients work hard to follow the rules more diligently than others. No one ever claimed that overcoming pain would be easy, but the more determined you are to break old habits, the less prominently pain will feature in your life.

The Ten Commandments are important because they will be your daily mentor for the future. If you forget about them in six months or six years, you will go back to old pain-dominated ways. You may have taken the ideas of Pain Management on board mentally, but it takes time to undergo a physical conversion.

The situation, in fact, is not quite as daunting as it first appears because, in time, the more relaxed and physically fit you become, the easier the guidelines are to keep up. There is no doubt, however, that you still have a long road to travel before attaining a level of movement at which you do not have to consciously remember the ideas outlined in this book.

The Ten Commandments have no particular order of importance or priority, but each one must be absorbed as completely as possible into your new routine.

1 Accept That You Have Pain.

Your doctor and family probably accept that you have pain. By now, you know that it is not particularly useful to talk about it in the sense that you have to inform everyone that you are suffering. It does not help anyone – not your family, your friends, your doctor, your therapist – most of all yourself.

When other people come to accept your pain, it does not mean that they don't believe you are suffering. You either have pain, or you haven't. There is no such concept as imaginary pain. Pain is an emotional experience. Just as you experience happiness or depression, it is real and there is no question of it being imaginary.

Once you, and those around you, accept that you have pain it is important not to waste time shopping for a cure. Many people waste their lives trawling from doctor to doctor instead of diverting their energy into positive living. We do not live in a perfect world and there is not yet a cure for everything – especially your own particular pain. If there was, then there is every chance you would not be reading this book or attending a Pain Management Programme. Once you begin to search outside yourself for ways of getting better, the possibility of being disappointed increases. Research on patients attending the Pain Management Programme show that it is extremely rare for anyone to find a 'cure' by visiting consultant after consultant.

Accepting that you have pain means doing something about it by concentrating your efforts within yourself. Learn to ration the valuable energy that pain tries to drain away from you. If your pain should change, then by all means review the situation with your doctor or specialist. Every few years, it is worth having a chat with your doctor to ask if there are new developments which may improve your condition.

There may be a new carbon fibre implant to cure your bad back but, equally, there is the likelihood that no help is available. If there is a possibility of new treatment, always ask what the risks are, but never channel all your energy into clutching at medical straws.

If your specialist says that he is still unable to help you, wondering how you can find someone else who can is not a sensible option. Accepting pain means that you are the only person who can do something about it. If you have been shopping from doctor to doctor for years, this may be your final chance.

2 Set Regular Targets and Goals – and Make Sure You Achieve Them.

Setting targets is very important. To make progress, you must set them regularly, rather than rarely. They can be quite simple goals to achieve and need not even relate directly to your pain – washing your hair, keeping up your exercises, walking to the post office to post a letter. Allocate different targets to different days, with weekly goals, such as visiting a relative, going to church, or taking a walk to the pub.

The secret of setting targets is never to be vague about them. Decide what you are going to achieve each day and when you are going to do it. A week can quickly slide by in dreams and indecision without anything being attained.

It is good to have long-term targets, too – you may, for example, plan to return to work within six months or a year – but never leave them vague and open-ended. Break down each long term goal and think carefully about what going back to work may entail: it may require the ability to sit in a chair for four hours, to walk several hundreds yards, to be able to lift a certain weight. Build towards your big target by achieving individual goals along the way.

It is also important to avoid extremes. If, on one hand, you fail to set targets, you will never make progress at all; if you set particularly difficult ones, the chances are that you will fail.

It is easy to fall into the trap of being too stubborn, or too optimistic, and setting yourself tasks which prove impossible to achieve. Failure causes fear and depression, which lead back to the familiar, downward spiral of pain.

Set easy, simple targets which you know you can accomplish and do the best you can. List your goals and work methodically through them. If one or two prove hard to achieve, they can be a good indication that you are adopting the right approach. If you consistently achieve a 100 per cent

have to adopt to reduce pain and, because of this, time spent on any kind of 'body maintenance' is essential. Many of the world's older cultures embody this idea in one form or another. Indians who practice yoga – a combination of light exercise, relaxation and philosophy – are generally healthier than Westerners and suffer fewer muscle spasm-induced disorders and stress-induced diseases.

As you become more proficient at relaxation, you can spend less time at it. Some people learn how to put themselves in a light trance almost immediately. As time goes on, you can acquire the ability to relax in the most difficult of circumstances.

Relaxation is not just for pain, but for every aspect of daily living. Half an hour spent relaxing each day will give a good return: there is evidence to show that people who relax regularly live longer and more healthy lives.

5 Take Your Analgesics on a Time Basis, Reducing Them Whenever Possible.

Simple painkillers are fine as long as you do not suffer side-effects. Aspirin, Panadol and anything that can be bought across the counter (especially anything that ends in 'fen', such as Nurofen, Brufen, Ibuprofen etc) are quite acceptable – as long as they do not make you suffer in other ways.

When you move up to codeine-based compounds on the analgesic ladder, much more care is required. These drugs tend to be reasonably efficient for a week or two, but then restrict the body from producing endorphins. The danger lies when you stop taking the tablets. Pain returns, not because the disease is worse, but because your body is telling you it wants tablets instead of producing its own endorphins.

We all need endorphins, simply because our bodies and

brains cannot function without them. If you stop making your own because you are taking something that imitates them, your endorphin factory will shut down production. Unfortunately, after some months of this, the blueprint becomes lost. When the substitute endorphins fail to appear, the body is unable to produce its own supply because it has forgotten how to.

Drug addicts who take morphine, the next rung on the analgesic ladder, face similar withdrawal symptoms. They suffer severe abdominal pain, even though there may be nothing physically wrong with them. If you have a problem with your back or leg and take morphine-like drugs, when you stop them you will have pain. If the pain comes when you are due to take your next tablet, it may indicate that you have a drug habit because you are not producing your own endorphins.

When you reduce this kind of medication, it is better to take tablets according to the clock, not according to the pain. The more often you take them when the pain dictates, the more your brain will believe you need tablets when the pain is bad and turn up the pain volume to demand more. Try to dissociate the taking of drugs from the intensity of the pain. If your pain becomes worse, try not to take more tablets than you had already planned, otherwise it becomes increasingly difficult to break the cycle.

6 Remember and Understand the Psychological Factors Maintaining Your Pain, and What You Can do to Prevent Them From Making Your Pain Worse.

Because pain is a psychological experience, psychological factors will make it worse, keep it going or influence it in some way. The factors differ and vary from person to person.

It may be that the subconscious is maintaining pain for reasons buried in the distant past. This happened in the cases of the patients described on pages 142 and 145.

Another psychological factor is using pain as an excuse to get out of doing something you do not enjoy. Once you do this, the situation always rebounds on you. People then complain that pain stops them from doing things they enjoy, as well as the things they dislike.

It is important to study yourself closely and discover exactly what makes the pain worse. Understanding the psychological aspects of your problem can modify your life and help you to accomplish more.

7 Get Angry With Your Pain if it Seems to be Getting the Upper Hand.

Anger is a negative emotion and has to be handled carefully, but only because we generally use it in the wrong way. It is easy for someone to feel angry with a doctor because they have been sold the idea that medicine can make everyone better. They are angry because no one can help them, but there is little point to it. The doctor has not failed because he does not want to help.

Similarly, some people get angry with doctors who have caused them pain. This is understandable, but it is not useful. When you become angry, frustrated and tense, it serves only to make the pain worse.

People get angry with their families for not understanding enough about them, or failing to cope with them. Indeed, one of the worst things about chronic pain is that it makes people irritatable and tetchy. But it is no use getting angry with someone else. You have to train yourself to be more controlled. Rehearse in your mind what makes you snap when your family says something. After all, it is not they who caused your pain.

Most importantly, never be angry with yourself. When you see other people coping well with their pain and making progress, you should not feel angry about how difficult you find things. Everyone moves at their own pace. The answer is not to feel angry about your lack of progress, but to keep going.

Try getting angry with your pain instead. Focus all your energy on the pain, on the sole thing that everyone dislikes. When you feel your emotions rise, tunnel them down onto your pain and make your anger shrink it. This can actually be done and is a useful way to channel negative emotions so that they do not rebound off those around you.

8 Get Your Family and Friends to Reinforce Your Positive Action – Not Your Pain and Disability.

Here, we are back to Pavlov's dogs again. Whenever Pavlov gave his dogs a meal, he rang a bell. After a few days the dogs associated the bell with being fed. When the bell rang, they salivated on cue. Once this kind of conditioning behaviour is established you no longer have to reinforce the sound of the bell with food to make the dogs drool. Like many things in life, such as speaking with an accent, it becomes a conditioned response.

When people reinforce your illness, they condition you to being ill. Every time you do something and they step in to help because they think it will make you ill, they condition you to become an invalid. Continue this for long enough and you will remain an invalid, long after the original problem has gone away.

Your family have to learn to ignore you more kindly or to help in a positive way by creating time and space for exercise and relaxation. Family and friends should encourage you to be well. If someone has been complaining about pain for 20 years and suddenly does something positive, that is the time they should be paid the most attention.

Instead of rejecting your family's offers of help, explain to them that it has to be constructive for you to improve mentally and physically. We all need the support of people around us, but only in the right way.

9 Remember That Working in a Group is More Fun and More Effective.

It is important to form links with others for exercise and relaxation, as well as social events. Being alone and in pain isn't much fun. When you have read this book you might feel that you do not want to associate with others who have chronic pain. High-fliers who return to work still need a group of some kind to communicate with. It is extremely difficult to sort out some problems by yourself.

The group you join does not have to be a pain group. You can join local classes for exercise or yoga. The important thing is that if you do not turn up for two weeks, someone will probably ring and ask if you are all right, or encourage you to return.

Social contact is one of the cornerstones of civilization. Isolating yourself is the worse thing you can do. As the song says, 'people need people' for help, advice and encouragement. Whatever exercise or relaxation you plan, always join a group of some kind to keep you going.

S.H.I.P. (Self Help In Pain) evolved in 1983 from the Pain Management Programme at Walton Hospital. As Secretary Beryl Cross explains: 'The course helped to alleviate the sense of isolation felt by chronic pain sufferers, particularly as they met people in the same position as themselves. However, once the course was over, there was nothing left but to try to continue on their own, which proved very difficult.'

S.H.I.P. was formed to continue group therapy with the idea that even one day a week was a better option than struggling alone. People who live too far away to attend the weekly two hour T'ai Chi session at Walton Hospital keep in touch by newsletter. Other S.H.I.P. groups have since been formed around the country as a means of mutual support, encouragement and exchange of information. A list of addresses can be found at the back of the book.

New groups are being formed every year and visits are often arranged to help members keep in touch on a more personal basis. The atmosphere at S.H.I.P. meetings is friendly and informal and there are many activities designed to bring people together and make their pain more manageable.

10 Think Positive.

This is not easy when the road to recovery often appears to be three steps forward and four steps back. You must be prepared for times when you seem to be making little progress. Instead of sitting around feeling depressed and wondering what went wrong, it is import to plan for such occasions. Revise your targets to prepare for the possibility that you may have to rest for a few days.

Giving up and throwing away all the work you have put in and the progress you have made is the easy option. No one ever said that achieving a normal life again would be easy. When times are bad, you have to be positive and take pride in all your achievements.

If you work on all of the Ten Commandments you may receive benefit for a short period or a tremendous improvement which remains with you for the rest of your life. Some chronic pain patients have rebuilt their lives and become more physically active than ever before.

Not everyone can do as well as Mike Spring who overcame painful paralysis to build his own boat and sail single-handed to the Azores. But there are many unsung pain heroes who quietly rebuild their lives. It is appropriate to conclude with one of them – the story of a 59-year-old man named Arthur, who suffered severe pain below an operation scar for six years.

Any walking caused muscle spasm and made Arthur's pain worse. He was unable to play golf or to follow his hobby of gardening, because he could not dig. Intensive treatment at another Pain Clinic had failed to reduce his discomfort and allow him to return to work.

Arthur arrived at Walton Hospital's Pain Management Programme in May 1992. He was taking 20 tablets of various kinds each day. As well as difficulty in walking, he could not climb stairs, was unable to sit for more than a few minutes and found concentration almost impossible.

At the start of the Programme Arthur realized that the object was not to get rid of his pain, but to show him how to live with it. He took the idea on board and pressed himself into forming a firm opinion that '*this will work*'.

He stopped taking his tablets and soon felt considerably better. After just one week his quality of life had improved enormously. His thinking became positive and, within a short time, he felt that he had his life under control again. The pain was no longer getting the better of him – he felt that he was finally in charge of the way it affected his life.

After the Programme, he did not feel a need for drugs and his thinking was much clearer. He felt far less moody, he could move around better and actively enjoyed his new lifestyle.

Arthur still does exercises every day and puts aside a period for relaxation, which he now finds easy to do. His pain has certainly not gone away, but he is confident of having more control of its effect on him. Arthur also discovered that, as one becomes older, one's body changes and it is not unusual to have aches and pains. He feels it is important not to confuse the two and to blame all your shortcomings on chronic pain.

He has since returned to work, climbs stairs and plays golf regularly. The pain is still there, but he now has a quality of life which was not present before.

Arthur's success story is the kind we expect of people who follow the advice outlined in this book. With the right attitude, the future is not bleak. The opportunities are there and the possibilities enormous – providing you have the hope and the will to keep going.

Best wishes for success.

> 'For all the happiness mankind can gain, is not in pleasure, but in rest from pain.'
>
> Dryden

Appendices

DRUGS YOU MAY BE TAKING

If you are taking regular medication, look up the name of the drug in the lists below. It may help to find which rung of the analgesic ladder your doctor has placed you on.

Simple Analgesics

Some medications on this list, such as Veganin, are combinations. They are classified as simple analgesics because aspirin is the main ingredient.

ASPIRIN: containing aspirin or acetylsalic acid. *Trade Names*: Aspirin BPC Mixture, Analgesic Dellipsoids D6, Anodyne Dellipsoids D4, Asagran, Bayer Aspirin, Breoprin, Caprin, Hypon, Laboprin, Levius, Nu-seals, Paynocil, Safapryn, Trancoprin, Veganin, Bi-prin, Codral Junior, Ecotrin, Elsprin, Novespin, Prodol, Provoprin, Rhusal, Sedalgin, Solusal, SRA, Winsprin, Acetophen, Asadrine C-200, Astrin, Coryphen, Entrophen, Neopirine-25, Nova-Phase, Novasen, Rhonal, Sal-Adult, Sal-Infant, Supasa, Triaphen-10, Aquaprin, Aspasol, Aspegic, Anadin, Aspav.

SOLUBLE ASPIRIN. *Trade Names*: Disprin, Antoin, Aspar, Claradin, Codis, Migravess, Myolgin, Solprin. *Buffered or* *with antacid*: Aloxiprin, Palaprin (Paloxin S.A.), Trisilate, Doloxene Compound, Equagesic, Hypon, Laboprin, Migress, Robaxisal Forte.

PARACETAMOL. *Trade Names*: Panadol, Acetaminophen, Cafadol, Calpol, Dimotapp, Disprol, Dolvan, Lobak, Medised Suspension, Medocodene, Myolgin, Neurodyne, Norgesic, Paldesic, Pamol, Panadeine, Panasorb, Paracodol, Paradeine, Parahypon, Parake, Paralgin, Paramax, Paramol, Para-selzer, Pardale, Paxidal, Pharmidone, Propain, Salzone, Solpadeine, Syndol, Ticelgesic, Tinol, Unigesic, Bramcetamol, Calpon, Ceetamol, Dolamin, Dymadon, Pacemol, Panamax, Paracet, Parasin, Paraspen, Parmol, Placemol, Tempra, Atasol, Campain, Exdol, Robigesic, Rounox, Tivrin, Tylenol, Ennagesic, Fevamol, Napamol, Paraprom, Pyralen, Repamol, Sedapyren.

PARACETAMOL IN COMBINATION WITH ASPIRIN. *Trade Names*: Benorylate, Benoral, Winolate.

NSAIDs

AZAPROPAZONE. *Trade Names*: Rheumox, Prolix.

BENZYDAMINE. *Trade Names*: Difflam Cream or Rinse, Tantum.

BUFEXAMAC. *Trade Names*: Parfenac Cream, Paraderm, Norfemac, Audax Eardrops.

CHOLINE SALICYLATE. *Trade Names*: Bonjela or Teejel mouth gels. Arthropan.

DICLOFENAC. *Trade Name*: Voltarol.

DIFLUNISAL. *Trade Name*: Dolobid.

FENBUFEN. *Trade Names*: Lederfen, Cinopal.

FENOPROFEN. *Trade Names*: Fenopron, Progesic.

FLUFENAMIC ACID. *Trade Names*: Meralen, Arlef.

FLURBIPROFEN. *Trade Name*: Froben.

IBUPROFEN. *Trade Names*: Apsifen, Brufen, Ebufac, Fenbid, Ibusio, Ibumetin, Lidifen, Motrin, Nurofen, Paxofen, Inoven, Seminax.

INDOMETHACIN. *Trade Names*: Artracin, Imbrilon, Indocid, Indoflex, Indolar, Indomod, Mobilan, Rheumacin, Arthrexin.

INDOPROFEN. *Trade Name*: Flosint.

KETOPROFEN. *Trade Names*: Alrheumat, Orudis, Oruvail.

MEFENAMIC ACID. *Trade Names*: Ponstan, Ponstan Forte.

METHYL SALICYLATE OINTMENTS & CREAMS. *Trade Names*: Oil of Wintergreen, Balmosa, Bengue's Balsam, Dubam.

NAPROXEN SODIUM. *Trade Names*: Naprosyn, Synflex, Laraflex.

NEFOPAM. *Trade name*: Acupan.

OXPHENBUTAZONE. *Trade Names*: Tandacote, Tandalgesic, Tanderil, Oxbutazone, Tandearil, Artzone, Buteril, Fibutrox, Otone.

PHENYLBUTAZONE. *Trade Names*: Butacote, Butazolidine, Butazone, Parazolidin, Tributazone, Butacal, Buratex, Butoroid, Butoz, Buzon, Algoverine, Butagesic, Intrabutazone, Malgesic, Nadozone, Neo-Zoline, Phenbutazone, Butrex, Panazone.

PHENAZONE. *Trade Names*: Auralgicin, Auraltone, Sedonan.

PHENAZOPYRIDINE. *Trade Names*: Pyridium, Phenazo, Azodine.

PIROXICAM. *Trade Name*: Feldene.

SALSALATE. *Trade Name*: Discalcid.

SODIUM SALICYLATE. *Trade Names*: Entrosalyl, Ancosal, Ensalate, Rheumax.

SULINDAC. *Trade Name*: Clinoril.

TOLMETIN. *Trade Names*: Tolectin, Tolectin DS.

SUPROFEN. *Trade Name*: Suprol.

MORAZONE. *Trade Name*: Delimon.

TIAPROFENIC ACID. *Trade Name*: Surgam.

ETODOLAC. *Trade Names*: Ramadar, Lodine.

ALOXIPRIN. *Trade Names*: Pelaprin.

Useful addresses

GREAT BRITAIN

The Pain Relief Foundation
Rice Lane
Liverpool L9 1AE
Tel: 0151 523 1486

The National Back Pain Association
16 Elmtree Road
Teddington
Middlesex TW11 8ST
Tel: 0181 977 5474
Or Edinburgh: 0131 667 0594

Arthritis Care
6 Grosvenor Crescent
London SW1X 7ER
Tel: (Help-line, Mon-Fri: 1pm – 5pm) 0800 289 170

Arthritis & Rheumatism Council For Research
PO Box 177
Chesterfield
Derbyshire S41 7TQ
Tel: 01246 558033

British Heart Foundation
14 Fitzhardinge Street
London W1H 4DH
Tel: 0171 935 0185

The Migraine Trust
45 Great Ormond Street
London WC1N 3HZ
Tel: 0171 278 2676

REMAP (Free advice service for adapting appliances to ease the problem of daily living)
Hazeldean
Ightham
Sevenoaks
Kent TN15 9AD
Tel: 01732 883818

COMPLEMENTARY THERAPIES

Relaxation for Living
12 New Street
Chipping Norton
Oxon 0X7 5LJ
Tel: 01608 646100

Society of Alexander Technique Teachers
10 London House
266 Fulham Road
London SW10 9EL
Tel: 0171 351 0828

Chartered Society of Physiotherapy
14 Bedford Row
London WC1R 4ED
Tel: 0171 242 1941

National Federation of Spiritual Healers
Old Manor Farm Studio
Church Street
Sunbury-on-Thames
Middlesex TW16 6RG
Tel: 01932 783164/5

General Council and Register of Osteopaths
St Jame's Square
London SW1Y 4JH
Tel: 0171 839 2060

British Chiropractic Association
29 Whitley Street
Reading
Berkshire RG2 0EG
Tel: 01734 757 557

British Acupuncture Council
Park House
604 Latimer Road
London W10 6RE
Tel: 0181 964 0222

COUNSELLING AND WELFARE SERVICES

S.P.O.D. (Association to aid the sexual and personal relationships of people with a disability)
286 Camden Road
London N7 0BJ
Tel: 0171 607 8851

RELATE (Marriage Guidance Council)
Check your local phone directory or Citizens' Advice Bureau for RELATE in your area.

Cancer Aftercare & Rehabilitation Society
Lodge Cottage
Church Lane
Timsbury
Bath BA3 1LF

Unwind (Tape-contact club for sufferers of emotional and physical pain)
Marie Langley
3 Alderlea Close
Durham DH1 1DS

SELF-HELP IN PAIN GROUP

S.H.I.P.
Room 27 (Old Sewing Room)
Walton Hospital
Rice Lane
Liverpool L9 1AE

Pain Concern UK
PO Box 318
Canterbury
Kent CT2 0GD

P.I.P. (People In Pain)
Mrs. E. Cottam
White Gables
The Green
Wrea Green
Preston
Lancashire PR4 2WO

Cymorth Mewn Poen
Suzanne Fisher
1 Caeau Gleision
Rhiwlas
Bangor
Gwynedd
North Wales LL57 4EW

S.H.I.P. Devon
Sandra Harrup
28 Salisbury Road
Exmouth EX8 1SL

UNITED STATES

Acupuncture International Association
2330 South Brentwood Boulevard
St. Louis
MO 63144

American Guild of Hypnotherapists
7117 Farnham Street
Omaha
NE 68132

American Heart Association
7320 Greenville Avenue
Dallas
TX 75231

American Osteopathic Association
212 East Ohio Street
Chicago
IL 60611

American Pain Society
340 Kingsland Street
Nutley
NJ 17110

American Rheumatism Association
3400 Peachtree Road
NE Atlanta
GA 30326

American Society of Clinical Hypnosis
2250 East Devon Avenue
Suite 336
Des Plains
IL 60018

Biofeedback Society of America
4301 Owens Street
Wheat Ridge
CO 80033

International Association for the Study of Pain
Westlund Building
Room 301
1309 Summit Avenue
Seattle
WA 98101

National Committee on the Treatment of Intractable Pain
PO Box 9553
Friendship Station
Washington
DC 20016

National Migraine Foundation
5252 North Western Avenue
Chicago
IL 60625

CANADA

Acupuncture Foundation of Canada
10 St. Mary Street
Toronto, ON
M4Y 1P9

Arthritis Society
1129 Carling Avenue
Ottawa, ON
K1Y 4G6

Arthritis Society
895 West Tenth Avenue
Vancouver, BC
V5Z 1L7

Arthritis Society
920 Yonge Street
Toronto, ON
M4W 3C7

Canadian Heart Foundation
1 Nicholas Street
Suite 1200
Ottawa, ON
K1N 7B7

Canadian Osteopathic Aid Society
575 Waterloo Street
London, ON
N6B 2R2

Canadian Physiotherapy Association
44 Eglinton Avenue West
Suite 201
Toronto, ON
MR4 1A1

L'Institut International Du Stress
659 Hilton Street
Montreal, PQ
H2X 1W6

Migraine Foundation
390 Brunswick Street
Toronto, ON
M5R 2Z4

Ontario Osteopathic Society
45 Richmond Street West
Suite 401
Toronto, ON
M5H 1Z2

AUSTRALIA

Arthritis and Rheumatism Council
Wynyard House
291 George Street
Sydney
NSW 2000

Biofeedback Meditation Relaxation Centre
165 Adderton Road
Carlingford
NSW 2118

Canberra Arthritis and Rheumatism Association
PO Box 352
Woden
ACT 2806

National Heart Foundation of Australia
55 Townshend Street
Phillip
ACT 2606

NEW ZEALAND

Arthritis and Rheumatism Foundation of New Zealand
PO Box 10-020
Southern Cross Building Brandon Street
Wellington

National Heart Foundation of New Zealand
17 Great South Road
Newmarket
PO Box 17128
Green Lane
Auckland 5

SOUTH AFRICA

National Heart Effort
PO Box 70
Tygerberg

South Africa Rheumatism and Arthritis Association
Namaquq House
36 Burg Street
Capetown 8001

Recommended reading

Aquarobics – Glenda Baum (Arrow)

The Challenge of Pain – Melzack & Wall (Penguin)

The Complete Hip and Thigh Diet – Rosemary Conley (Arrow)

Conquering Pain – Dr Sampson Lipton (Methuen)

Coping Successfully With Pain – Neville Shone (Sheldon Press, London)

Drug Free Pain Relief – Dr George Lewith & Sandra Horn (Thorsons)

Games People Play – Eric Berne [The Psychology of Human Relationships] (Penguin)

Medicine – The Self-Help Guide – Professor Michael Orme & Dr Suzanna Graham-Jones (Viking)

The Puzzle of Pain – Melzack & Wall (Penguin)

The Reader's Digest Guide to Alternative Medicine (Consumers' Association)

Understanding Back Trouble – (Consumers' Association/ Hodder)

Understanding Stress – (Consumers' Association/Hodder)

Useful tapes

The Relaxation Kit (65 Minutes). A collection of four different relaxation programmes used at The Walton Centre for pain relief. £13.99 including postage and packing.

Feeling Good (72 Minutes). Two strategies for helping those with chronic pain regain their slef-esteem and assertiveness skills. £13.99 including post and packing.

Coping With Pain (40 Minutes). Techniques and strategies for coping with pain on a daily basis. Presented by Magnus Magnusson. £8.50 including post and packing.

Coping With Back Pain – Dr Sampson Lipton (Methuen)

Coping Successfully With Pain (70 Minutes). Effective techniques and simple exercises for coping with back pain. Includes 20 minute relaxation programme. £13.99 including post and packing.

Coping With Headaches and Migraine (40 Minutes). How to cope with and avoid headaches and migraines. Including a Visualisation Relaxation Programme. £8.50 including post and packing.

All the above tapes are available from: Wendy Lloyd Audio Productions Ltd, PO Box, Wirral, L47 7DD or telephone 0151- 632-0662

Index

Other back titles available from

VERMILION

SHIATSU

An introductory guide to the technique and its benefits

Ray Ridolfi

Shiatsu is a Japanese word meaning 'finger pressure' and is sometimes referred to in the West as 'acupressure'. Like acupuncture and aromatherapy, shiatsu aims to balance the body's energies and it works on the principle that healing touch can trigger self-healing in the patient. It has been effectively used in Eastern medicine for several thousand years.

In this book Ray Ridolfi explains what to expect from a course of treatment, and gives specific advice on the types of condition that can benefit from shiatsu. This straightforward guide answers all your questions about shiatsu as well as providing background information on this increasingly popular treatment.

THE COMPLETE GUIDE TO GOOD POSTURE AT WORK

The self-help manual for sufferers of back and neck pain, RSI and other related conditions

Andrew Wilson

This book explores the effects of poor posture and repetitive strain on our health - with particular reference to work practices. Half the population spend 70% of their day sitting down and the way we sit can result in tension headaches, lower back pain, stiff neck and shoulders and many other ailments.

This beneficial book illustrates how simple changes to our working environment can help us become more physically efficient and alleviate health problems. With simple, clearly explained ideas for transforming our working area, self-help exercises and advice on the latest health and saftey regulations, this is the definitive guide to alleviating and preventing problems caused by incorrect posture.

Ψ

To order your copy direct from Vermilion, use the form below or call TBS DIRECT on **01621 819596.**

Please send me

......copies of **SHIATSU @ £5.99** each

......copies of **THE COMPLETE GUIDE TO GOOD POSTURE AT WORK @ £8.99** each

Mr/Ms/Mrs/Miss/Other (BlockLetters)

....

Address..

....

....

Postcode...............................Signed.............................

HOW TO PAY

☐ I enclose a cheque/postal order for £........................
made payable to 'Tiptree Book Services'

☐ I wish to pay by Access/Visa/Switch/Delta card (delete where appropriate)

Card Number ☐☐☐☐☐☐☐☐☐☐☐☐☐☐☐☐☐☐☐☐

Expiry Date ☐☐☐☐

Post order to **TBS Direct, Tiptree Book Services, St. Lukes Chase, Tiptree, Essex, CO5 0SR.**

POSTAGE AND PACKING ARE FREE. Offer open in Great Britain including Northern Ireland. Books should arrive less than 28 days after we receive your order; they are subject to availability at time of ordering. If not entirely satisfied return in the same packaging and condition as received with a covering letter within 7 days. Vermilion books are available from all good booksellers.